Reflecting on the Grave and the Bones within:
A Locus for Individual Will, Action and Identity

Marina Pinto

BAR International Series 2425

2012

Published in 2016 by
BAR Publishing, Oxford

BAR International Series 2425

Reflecting on the Grave and the Bones within: A Locus for Individual Will, Action and Identity

ISBN 978 1 4073 1024 4

BAR Publishing is the trading name of British Archaeological Reports (Oxford) Ltd.
British Archaeological Reports was first incorporated in 1974 to publish the BAR
Series, International and British. In 1992 Hadrian Books Ltd became part of the BAR
group. This volume was originally published by Archaeopress in conjunction with
British Archaeological Reports (Oxford) Ltd / Hadrian Books Ltd, the Series principal
publisher, in 2012. This present volume is published by BAR Publishing, 2016.

Printed in England

BAR
PUBLISHING

BAR titles are available from:

BAR Publishing
122 Banbury Rd, Oxford, OX2 7BP, UK
EMAIL   info@barpublishing.com
PHONE   +44 (0)1865 310431
FAX   +44 (0)1865 316916
www.barpublishing.com

ACKNOWLEDGEMENTS

A book like this one is always the product of many minds and hearts even though it is credited to a sole author. The present work is no exception. I am indebted first and foremost to Wenner-Gren (Grant No. 5357), for supporting my documentary research in Madrid and Seville, without which this work would not have been possible.

I extend my deepest gratitude to friends and family in Spain who most generously extended their hospitality to me. My stay in Madrid was made possible by Dr. and Mrs. Pedro Sauret and my cousins Jesus Cruces Pinto and Inmaculada Estepa. Getting around on my own was a daunting prospect given my dependence on crutches for walking, but welcome assistance was always forthcoming.

I am very grateful to the staff at the Archivo de Protocólos in Madrid for their extraordinary warmth and helpfulness towards me not only in matters of retrieving the documents I requested, but also in escorting me in and out of an inaccessible building every day. I also offer my sincerest thanks to all of the staff at the Biblioteca Nacional, the Museo Nacional de Arqueología, and the Instituto Arqueológico Alemán for their consideration in similar matters. I could not have done without them.

I cannot forget the people at the Archivo Histórico Provincial de Sevilla, neither the archivists nor the maintenance staff. Had it not been for their timely intervention, I would not have been able to contact the Director of the archive in order to obtain permission to examine documents that were otherwise off-limits to all researchers. Thanks to all of them I was given a unique opportunity to study the entire series of fifteenth century wills in their collection.

I also owe a great deal to my friends and fellow scholars while in Madrid and Seville, most notably Elena Sanchez de Madariaga, Linda Curcio and Chris von Nagy. Elena shared many documents that she thought might be of interest for my work. She also introduced me to the archive director at the church of San Gines who gave me access to bills of sale of burial plots in the church that I would otherwise never have encountered. Linda and Chris were also most helpful in reminding me of the anthropology that should inform my research even as I was steeped in the pursuit of historical data. Among many others whose contributions are not forgotten are Emilio and Ines González Grano de Oro, Peter Cherry, Iris Gareis, Charlene Black and Line Amselem for their wonderful friendship, advice, and support on various aspects of the experience of archival research itself.

On a similar note, I could not have done without the unstinting support, critical advice and great generosity of Dr. James Amelang, who gave freely of his time and expertise during my stay in Spain. His continued interest in my progress since then has been a source of inspiration to me, especially during those periods when I felt I had lost direction. I extend the same heartfelt gratitude to my other advisors and friends, most especially to Dr. Victoria Bricker, Dr. Elizabeth Graham, and Edward F. Maeder. Without their extensive and detailed feedback on professional and sometimes very personal issues connected with the book, I would not have been able to complete the present work.

Grateful thanks also go to Paul Odette, who very patiently and diligently worked with me to create a database for the enormous amount of textual information that I had accumulated during my sojourn in Spain. His ever-present kindness, consideration and good humour, despite my difficulties in understanding the requirements of programming, remain invaluable to me.

Last, but never least, I cannot forget my father and mother, Ricardo and Susan Pinto, my family and all my friends who have, over the years, shared the joys and grief of this work with me. I thank them for their faith in me, their endless patience, and for their many efforts to "will me along" even as my spirits soared and sank on this long quest. Their constant love and support is the only truly lasting groundwork for everything that I might hope to achieve in these pages. No words of thanks suffice other than to say that I dedicate the present work to all of them, both the living and the dead.

TABLE OF CONTENTS

List of Tables

Table

List of Figures

Figure

List of Abbreviations

AHPM   Archivo Histórico de Protocólos de Madrid
AHPS   Archivo Histórico Provincial de Sevilla

Editorial Note

The placement of accents on Spanish names and words cited in the text, appendices, end notes and references cited is a compromise between modern usage and standard practice in paleographic transcription of texts that pre-date the introduction of such usage. I have followed modern usage in citing Spanish titles of recent publications and archaeological site names.

Place and personal names are also accented according to modern usage, unless they appear in transcription in the endnotes or in translation in the text from the sixteenth or seventeenth century original. Testators' names and those of the people, places and things they mention are given as they appear in the wills, with accents, (or lack thereof) and orthography preserved intact.

CHAPTER 1. INTRODUCTION

The work that I now lay before you is an experiment. It is anchored by newly recovered documentary data, but it takes its character from two conditions set by me. The first is a recognition of the potential of historical documents to provide answers to questions raised in archaeological excavation that cannot be answered by archaeology alone. The second is an intimate familiarity with the last wills of well over a thousand souls who lived and died in Madrid and Seville from the late fifteenth through the early seventeenth centuries. The archives of these cities were chosen because they contain the largest extant collections of wills written in Spanish for the period. I draw from transcriptions of selected portions of 1038 wills, consulted at the Archivo Histórico de Protocólos in Madrid, that date from 1503 through 1630. The remainder of my sample of transcriptions comes from the Archivo Histórico Provincial in Seville, where I examined 188 wills dating from 1450 to 1498.

Genesis of the Present Work

The impetus for my investigation came from what I expected to find in wills that could not be obtained in full from any other source. I wanted to acquire a body of data on grave location that encompassed what people say in their wills (those who leave wills are henceforth referred to as testators), about where they want to be buried upon their death. In keeping with my archaeological training, I focused on mention of defined exterior and interior spaces; objects and the bodies of those already laid to rest. Is it a church, a monastery, an outdoor cemetery or an indoor chapel and what is it called? Is some other feature, such as a door, a window or an altar named within the church as well? Does the testator make reference to the use of a gravestone, a coffin, a shroud or any other material artifact associated with the funeral and interment? Is there someone who he or she is inclined to lie next to, or join in the same grave when the hour has come? Such were the questions that I asked of the documents I read.

I sought to confirm what a Spanish Christian burial of the sixteenth century would look like, when considered from above and below ground. To this end I also collected all the information I could find on the excavation of medieval and early modern period churches, churchyard cemeteries and necropoli in Spain, some of which are cited where appropriate in ensuing pages. I was eager to know: what of this ensemble of information might remain intact in archaeological contexts of the Old and the New Worlds at the inception of Spanish contact and colonization of the Americas?

My early initiative and ideas were prompted by excavation of the Colonial Period site of Tipu, located on the Macal River in southwestern Belize (Graham 1993). I was struck by the fact that the inhabitants of this frontier Maya town appeared to have adopted a Christian mode of burial. Some 627 burials were unearthed from graves inside the church and in the cemetery adjacent to it, (Graham, personal communication). Without exception, all individuals interred at Tipu were of Maya, not European ancestry. Yet in the vast majority of cases, the body of the deceased had been positioned to lie flat on the back with arms crossed on the chest or at the pelvis and the head oriented to the west and the feet to the east (Graham and Bennett 1989:8). Almost no grave goods, other than items of personal adornment, were in evidence, whereas grave furnishings were limited to shroud and coffin burial (1989:8).

Despite historical evidence suggesting a lack of sustained contact with Spanish missionaries and a prolonged period of rebellion against and independence from any Spanish political or military control (Jones 1988) a Spanish cultural practice seemed to have taken root among the Maya of Tipu. I shared this observation with many scholars in the fields of history, ethnohistory anthropology and archaeology, and was greatly encouraged to pursue the direction of my interest in the manner that I have described above. The substantive content of both the wills and the archaeological reports that I later consulted in

Spain confirm beyond doubt that the Maya at Tipu disposed of their dead according to a set of customs (belief is another question altogether, quite outside the scope of this work) that in a European or Spanish Colonial context, would be identified as Christian or Catholic.

Continued Development: New Insights and Information

The true story behind the development of my work really begins with what I found in the wills that I could never have anticipated before I actually encountered them. The range, complexity and particularity of what people say about themselves, their family, professional and religious networks, their beliefs and values, their financial resources and their social aspirations in relation to the deceptively simple question of where to be buried is staggering. My quest for references to specific objects, spaces, locales and categories of people in statements about burial location grew to include the context or "field of action" around preparations of the body for burial, the deployment of material and human resources for the funeral mass, accompaniment of the corpse and subsequent memorial services, in addition to the means of access to and the marking of the grave site itself.

In keeping with this expanded outlook, new information emerged from my reading and review of the wills that was to become instrumental in the formulation of the ideas that I present in the following chapters. A request to have one's body transferred from one place of interment to another at some time after death is just one of many possible examples of texts that went beyond my reductionist views of location. Every testator who makes a request of this sort talks about his or her selection of burial location in terms that may be contingent on family; finances; familiarity with a church, chapel, or altar devoted to a beloved saint; or incidental circumstances such as travel, or a sudden illness or idiosyncratic factors.

When I realized that the mention of any one or more of these conditions is at once a specific expression of location as much as it is an explanation of the decision to be buried in a particular place, I gained enormously on two fronts. This insight has enabled me to expand on standard approaches to the use of documents vis-a-vis archaeological investigation, in ways that I believe will have wider implications for both ethnohistory and archaeology. At the same time, it has altered the direction of my work and opened up interpretive possibilities that I could not have foreseen.

Purpose of My Work and Chapter Summary

The purpose of my work is to explore the information derived from wills in ways that expand on the possibilities for archaeological interpretation of grave sites without distorting the integrity of the texts of wills and site reports. Chapter 2 consists of a presentation of the specifics of testator's identity, the preparation of the body for burial and the selection of a grave location as these occur in the sample of wills. In Chapter 3 I go on to consider how some of this information may complement, or not, that derived from excavation of individual gravesites. Chapter 4 marks a shift from my earlier focus on content to an emphasis on perspective, through an exploration of archaeologists understanding of grave location as compared with that expressed in testators' statements about where their graves are. In the last two chapters I comment *in extenso* on the implications of selected texts for understanding the connection between action, identity and grave location and how all of this impinges on the material evidence, both positive and negative, that may be unearthed in excavation of grave sites. What is written in a will can give us greater insight into the identity and actions taken on behalf of the deceased, so that when we find a grave we may be able to draw some solid inferences about what once happened at that site, what once was there and what now remains.

Expanding on the Possibilities for Archaeological Interpretation of Grave Sites

My analysis allows archaeologists to step back and take note of how we approach key concepts such as space and location. We can appreciate how much our understanding of space is shaped by what we see in excavation. We are reminded of the gap between archaeological and living contexts. The wills yield many descriptive examples, which can be used to redress the balance.

Space and location may be summed up in the context of the wills as what the testator thinks it would take for someone to arrive at his or her grave site. The preceding observation is key to expanding on the possibilities for archaeological interpretation of grave sites because the same principle could be applied or perhaps tested in other cultural contexts with reference to other types of documents.

It touches on a piece of truth regarding documents of record that is universal - namely, that no text contained therein is arbitrary, incidental or insignificant and nothing is written unless it is seen to be necessary at the time of writing. By operating on this principle, I gain insight into how information about space and location is constructed in a real-world example - the necessity of finding a grave site - that is highly relevant to archaeological interests. In doing so, I draw closer to archaeology's aim of understanding a small piece of past human behavior in a very concrete way.

The wills also provide us with a repository of information concerning the will (intent) and prospective actions of over one thousand individuals with respect to grave site selection, the ultimate placement of the body and the use of material objects to commemorate the dead. My understanding that the sharpest distinction between the archaeologist's and testator's concepts of grave location lies in the area of identity - of grave and body - leads me to see the profound connection between action and identity.

All the information I need to support this connection is in the wills. In what follows, I present the view that *identity is the source of all human action in the world, and it is translated into physical space and time, by the exercise of individual will.* My analysis expands on the possibilities for archaeological interpretation of grave sites because I support this paradigm with examples of text that account for visible and material associations that we might encounter in excavation, or not, without setting up hard and fast generalizations.

CHAPTER 2. WILLS AS SOURCES OF INFORMATION ABOUT GRAVE SITES

In the present chapter I aim to provide an overview of the content and complexity of the information contained within these wills, so that the reader may become familiar with the context in which the argument of later chapters is based. The parameters of my subject matter are set by the terms of reference testators use to describe who they are, where their grave is or where they want it to be, and what material preparations they make for their bodies to be interred in the grave that they have chosen. The constituents of identity, location and a selected range of material objects are introduced here. They, along with many of the original texts from which they are taken, are the foil for all subsequent discussion of their counterparts, or lack thereof, that are available to us through archaeological excavation and interpretation of grave sites.

The possible contribution of testators' statements about where they want to be buried to archaeology or their placement within the historical context of fifteenth, sixteenth and seventeenth century Madrid and Seville is not my immediate concern here. The implications of many pieces of text require a degree of attention and documentation that goes well beyond the scope of my work.

I begin with a discussion of what is written in a will, focusing on those parts that I selected for transcription. I continue with a presentation of some of the key variables within my sample. Sex, marital status, the incidence of titles, university degrees and testators livelihoods or what I have termed professions, are variables relating to personal identity. Among the location specifiers associated with the disposition of the testator's body in a desired grave site are: the town in which the testator wishes to be buried, the building itself, sometimes the actual whereabouts of the grave within the building and finally, the identification of that plot as the grave of one's relatives. The last subset includes the frequency with which testators in my sample of wills request material items such as burial attire, coffins, and grave markers in relation to the disposition of their bodies in death.

What is Written in a Will

Invocation

The invocation comes first in the will. It is usually a standard phrase, sometimes a paragraph or more, in which the testator commends his or her soul to God and the saints. I did not record any of this information.

Date

Date refers to the day on which the will was drawn up. Unlike all other items in the present list, it occurs at the end, rather than at the beginning of the document. The date was given as day, month and year in the wills in Madrid. In the Seville sample the day of the week was also recorded.

Place

Place refers to the city or town, Madrid, Seville or a nearby village, where the testator lives. This is usually the same town in which the will is being drawn up.

Identity

Identity is composed of several pieces of information. At a minimum, the testator gives his or her name. Sometimes this includes mention of a form of address, a title of nobility or a university degree. All of these items precede the name itself. The testator's profession where specified follows his or her name. A woman is more likely to mention her marital status at this point and to name both her husband and his profession. A man may mention a wife here or later in the will in connection with her grave if he wants to be buried there, or in her capacity as executor of his will. Male testators' wives are less likely to be identified by name than are the husbands of female testators in my sample of wills.

State of Health

There is usually a standard phrase indicating that the testator was sound in mind and body at the time of making his or her will. I did not record it.

Disposition of Grave

As with identity, the disposition of the grave is a composite of many different pieces of information, not all of which are listed in every case. The name of the church, monastery, hospital or religious college where the testators' grave is, or is to be acquired by purchase or permission is most often the only indicator of grave location given. The name of the church is sometimes followed by mention of whose grave this is in cases where the testator is asking to be buried with a relative in the same plot or in a grave nearby.

Sometimes the testator may go on to elaborate the general locale of his or her grave and where it is in relation to the church, outside or in. If it is inside, some will go on to indicate the general area in which the grave is found or a desired location for it, such as in or near a chapel, in the choir, close to an altar, at the foot of a Holy Water stoup, a painting or religious image, in or next to a doorway or somewhere in relation to some other feature. In a few instances, the location of a grave is further specified by a description of where one or more of the above-mentioned features is in relation to the area in which it is placed. Gravestones, or any other identifying features of the plot itself, are mentioned at this juncture if at all. I recorded all of this information as it appeared in the wills.

Disposition of Body

Statements about where the grave is may be followed by a statement about how the body is to be dressed for burial, who is to accompany it to the grave, and whether or not it is to be buried in a coffin. I recorded all of this kind of information though I do not report all of it here.

The remainder of a will consists of requests for the care of the soul, the disposition of worldly goods, and finally the naming of executors. I did not pursue any information on masses, feast days, prayers, offerings, religious vocations, devotions to saints and the endowment and decoration of chapels unless some references to them were included in the few documents that I had photocopied at the archive. In later chapters I use most of the examples I have of text containing references to ritual activity, where it is appropriate to the discussion, but none of the material on such matters was ever incorporated into a sample built on select criteria.

Who is represented in the Sample of Wills

Number of Testators Represented in the Sample

There are 1227 wills in my sample of documents representing 1236 individuals in total. The discrepancy is made up by a total of twenty-eight testators in the sample. Seventeen men have joint wills with their wives and one brother with his sister, so thirty-six people are represented in eighteen wills. Another nine people in the sample, five men and four women have left two wills each. In addition, one man has three wills in the sample, all made several years apart and each one changed from the one written before it! Taken together, ten people account for twenty-one wills between them. Most of the counts presented below are based on the number of wills in the sample, rather than on the number of individuals represented in the wills. With the exception of testator's sex and marital status, no significant changes affecting any of the other samples were recorded for testators who had made joint wills or more than one will.

As to "who", testators are documented by several pieces of information not all of which are presented here. I have not discussed testators' names, places of origin, their parents or the parents of their spouses because such information is not relevant to my purpose. One's sex, marital status and to a more limited degree, titles and professions, are more directly expressed in testators statements about where, how and in whose grave they want to be buried.

Sex

The sample is evenly divided between both sexes. Six hundred thirty-two men and 602 women are represented in the wills. In two cases the testator's name was illegible and no information on gender was available.

Marital Status

Four different categories of marital status are distinguished in the wills: married, widowed, unmarried and those who do not specify any marital status at all. In all, 291 testators are widowed, 350 are married, 10 state that they are unmarried and 576 say nothing about their marital status at all.

Women are more likely to be specific about whether they are widowed, married or not than men are. Two hundred thirty-five women are widowed, as compared with fifty-six men. A further 249 women are married, while only 101 men claim the same status. All ten unmarried testators are women. Four hundred eighty-two men, in contrast to only 94 women, fail to specify their marital status.

Title or Degree

Here I present only the designations that exist in my sample as they appear in the original text of the will. I do not have enough information about the ramifications of each of these terms to go beyond a brief summary of their numerical distribution.

Only eleven people in the sample hold aristocratic titles: five counts, one countess and five Marquises. Ten men belong to military orders. Eight are members of the Order of Santiago, while two others are gentlemen of the orders of Alcántara and Calatrava respectively. With the exception of one Count of Salvatierra, who is also a member of the order of Alcántara there is no overlap between those who have aristocratic and those who have military titles.

Three university degrees are represented in the sample. Seven men call themselves "bachiller", four of whom are also clerics by profession. Nine men are "doctors". Four doctors also specify their profession. One is cathedral canon of the city of Valladolid, another is a jurist and the last two are medical doctor and chaplain to the King respectively. A similar spread of professions is indicated for the nineteen men who are "licenciados". Three are medical doctors to His Majesty, one is a surgeon, another is a lawyer, five are presbyters, one is a priest, and one is an archdeacon of the Inquisition in Seville.

Profession

A grand total of 375 testators in the sample name their profession. In addition, 200 others list the profession of a spouse. I can only approximate the meanings of many terms in the combined lists of professions, but in total 557 people occupy some 157 different professions. The meaning of eighteen entries is as yet undetermined. I do not have enough information to discuss any designations in detail. I note here however, that most people, 170 of 575, are involved in occupations that we would categorize as craft or fine art. Carpenters, bricklayers and tailors are the most frequently represented specialists, not only within this group but also in the entire sample.

Another 93 testators hold positions that are associated with King and court in Madrid. Almost half of this number 40 in total, are household servants. A further 61, mostly priests, clerics, a few chaplains and some members of regular orders, draw their living from the Church. Seventy-one testators in the sample describe themselves as laborers. The remainder of the sample consists of people who identify occupations in connection with medicine, law, trade and food. All of this information suggests that the majority of testators in the entire sample of 1227 people are ordinary people, drawn from all walks of life.

Where the Grave is in which the Body is to Lie

The question of where the grave in which the body is to lie may be represented best in the data by all possible references in the wills to the destination of the testator's body. Such references include the town, the physical setting (church or monastery), descriptors of grave location within the church or monastery and with whom the testator wants to be buried. Each of these components of testators' requests for burial in a certain locale is broken down into various samples as outlined below.

Locale in the Broadest Sense: What Town to be
Buried In

Five mutually exclusive subsets within the sample are based on locale in the broadest sense. Three subsets consist of testators who make wills and request burial in Madrid, in Seville and in towns other than Madrid and Seville respectively. In addition, some testators ask that their bodies be removed from a grave in one town to a preferred plot in another. The last subset of the sample includes testators who give more than one and sometimes more than two possible alternative locations for burial within the same town or in different towns.

I limit my focus to numerical distributions of testators' requests for burial in variously defined grave locations. None of the counts in each separate listing have been considered in relation to the date of the will or to one another, so none of the samples are mutually exclusive of one another unless they are defined by the same set of criteria. A testator, who requests burial in a church in Madrid for example, does not appear in the sample of testators who ask for a grave in a monastery in Seville.

Other samples discussed below are not discrete. For example, a testator who says he wants to be buried in his mothers grave, which happens to lie next to the altar, is counted in two samples presented below, that of burial with relatives and burial within a church or monastery setting. In addition, he is counted in the larger samples of towns, churches and monasteries. In other words my "samples" are indicative and relative, rather than definitive and comprehensive in nature.

Burial in Madrid

A combined total of 856 testators request burial in Madrid. 598 of this number want a grave in a church while 258 ask for a plot within monastery walls. In all, some seventeen churches and twenty-five monasteries are named as places of burial in Madrid. Numbers are approximate because the monastery of San Martin also served as a parish church, so I include it in both categories depending upon how it appeared in the original text of a testator's request for burial. Thirteen of the churches mentioned in Table 1 are parish churches, with the exceptions of San Gil, Casa de los Menores del Espiritu Santo and San Luis and San Myllan. Both the latter are annexed to the parishes of San Gines and San Yuste respectively.

Church Burial in Madrid

The numerical distribution of requests for burial in a specific church in Madrid may be described as follows. One church in the sample is listed as a desired place of burial over one hundred times. Two churches fall within the fifty to one hundred ranges. Most churches in the sample, eight in total, are cited somewhere between twenty-five and forty-eight times. One church appears less than twenty times and five receive mention less than ten times. Thirty-two testators fail to name a specific church and leave it to their executors to name one. I have counted these into the final total of church burials mentioned earlier but they do not appear in the table listed in the appendix.

Monastery Burial in Madrid

The numerical distribution of requests for burial in a specific monastery in Madrid is somewhat different from that of churches, with fewer people choosing from a larger range of options. Two monasteries are named thirty-one and sixty times respectively. Eight are cited somewhere between ten and twenty-one times. Nine monasteries fall within a range of two to nine mentions each. Five monasteries appear only once in the entire sample of 258 requests.

Burial in Seville

A combined total of 174 testators request burial in Seville. 122 of this number want a grave in a church while 52 ask for a plot within monastery walls. In all some eighteen churches and ten monasteries are named as places of burial in Seville.

Church Burial in Seville

The numerical distribution of requests for burial in a specific church in Seville may be described as follows. Four churches in the sample account for forty-eight requests between them, or over one third of the sample of 122 church burials. Three churches get six, eight and nine mentions respectively accounting for twenty-three requests. Another five churches are cited five times each for a combined total of twenty requests. The remaining five churches named in the sample are requested as places of burial only thirteen times altogether. Finally, thirteen testators fail to name a specific church and leave it to their executors to name one. Again as in the Madrid sample, I have counted these into the final total of church burials mentioned earlier but they do not appear in the table itself.

Monastery Burial in Seville

The numerical distribution of requests for burial in a specific monastery in Seville, as in Madrid, is skewed in favor of San Francisco, named twenty times in a sample of only fifty-two. Two monasteries between them account for nineteen more requests for burial, roughly half each. Two monasteries are cited three times each, another two appear twice and three others are mentioned only once. Seven monasteries account for the preferred gravesites of only thirteen testators altogether.

Burial in Places Other than Madrid and Seville

One hundred testators make their wills in small towns outside Madrid and Seville. They live and expect to die and be buried there. Eighty people ask to be buried in a local church and twenty others in monasteries.

Body Transfers

Thirty-nine testators request that their bodies be transferred from a temporary grave of deposit in a church or monastery to a final resting place in another location. Thirty-six testators ask that their bodies be transferred from Madrid to a grave in a distant town. Intervals of deposit are not specified but would have been long enough to permit the flesh to dry out or to leave only the bones prior to their removal for the last journey home.

Most testators who ask for body transfers want to be buried in a family plot or ancestral chapel in the place where they were born, with three exceptions. There is one instance of someone who wishes to be moved from his initial grave site to a more desirable plot within the same church of San Miguel de los Otoes in Madrid, when the building of a new chapel has been completed. Two testators ask that their remains be disinterred from the churches in which they are buried and moved to permanent gravesites in monasteries that are still under construction at the writing of their wills.

Alternative Locations for Burial

Twenty-six testators request burial in one church or monastery or another within the same town or in two different towns. Eleven name specific locales, depending on where they happen to die and where the graves containing different sets of relatives are located. Fifteen are premised on a "just in case scenario", relying largely on executors to make a final decision as to their final resting-place.

Burial within a Church or Monastery Setting

So far I have noted the incidence of testator's requests for burial in town, church and monastery. Another dimension of grave location is provided by testators' requests for burial in relation to a specific locale within a church or monastery setting. The content of this sample is not independent of the information already described above, but I present it now irrespective of the town, church or monastery in which the grave site is situated.

In all, 356 testators drawn from the sample of 1227 wills say something more about where to find the grave they want, than simply naming a particular building. Their plots are located inside or somewhere within the vicinity of a church or monastery, in a chapel, an altar, in or near the choir and the well remembered grave of a friend or acquaintance. They may be identified by proximity to doorways, to the stoup of Holy Water or because they are found within the nave of the church or in the sacred space to the right of the altar where the Gospel is spoken, or to the left of the altar, where the Epistles are read. The numerical distribution of the sample as I have described it here is given in Table 5.

Requests for Burial with Relatives and Others

One other dimension of grave location is provided by testators' requests for burial in the graves of relatives. A total of 592 testators in the sample of 1227 wills indicate a desire to be buried in the graves of family members, or in closest proximity with the graves of already deceased relatives.

Three hundred fifty-five of this number, want burial with one or more of their relatives by birth. Parents, grandparents, children, grandchildren, brothers, sisters, aunts and uncles are included in the category of birth relatives.

Two hundred others ask to be buried with family to which they are related by marriage. In-laws and spouses as well as any other members of a spouse's family are included within the category of relatives by marriage.

Only thirty-seven people, out of a total of 592, request burial in a grave with a person or persons to whom they are not or do not appear to be related by birth or marriage. Among this group are persons who are named, but whose exact relationship to the testator is not stated. The remainder consist of requests for burial with people with whom the testator is associated by profession or activity.

How they are Laid to Rest

The question of how a testator was laid to rest is used here in a broad sense to refer to material objects mentioned in the wills which have some bearing on the handling of the testator's body in the interval from death through burial. Requests for various kinds of burial attire, for the use of coffins in burial, or during funeral ceremonies, or not at all, and mention of stone or sculptured monuments to mark the grave make up the samples that I now describe.

Attire

Five hundred forty-one of testators make a specific request for burial in a piece of cloth or clothing acquired for that purpose. 208 of this number ask that their bodies be wrapped in a shroud. 333 others prefer to go to their graves dressed in a religious habit. Many different varieties of habit are named in the sample, including the habits of nine regular orders, a priests' garb and tunics that identify the wearer even in death as a member of a lay confraternity or a military order. Among those who ask to be buried in a habit of one of the regular orders are four testators who would make separate use of two different habits. In three of these four cases the use of a certain habit depends on which alternative location is finally selected as the testator's grave site. The last of these four testators asks to die dressed in one habit and to be buried in another.

Coffins

A total of eighty-three testators in the sample of 1227 wills mention a coffin in connection with their preparations for burial. Fifty-nine of the eighty-three ask to be buried in a coffin. Another twenty ask to be carried to the church in a coffin, without mention of burial in the same. Four testators ask that they be laid in the grave without a coffin.

Grave Markers

Only twenty-seven testators in the sample of 1227 include physical descriptions of a fixed marker created to identify their gravesites. Twenty-three testators allude to a grave stone. Thirteen of this number request that that a grave stone be placed on their graves, with an epitaph, usually their name, carved into it. Ten testators mention a gravestone that already marks their intended resting-place.

Four others describe the chapels they are building to house their graves. There are forty-five other testators in the sample of 1227 wills who request burial in a chapel owned, built or bought by a family relation. They are not considered part of the present sample because no reference to the form, material, design or appearance of any of these chapels is made.

Conclusion

The implications of the text move well beyond the type and quantity of the information that may be gleaned from archaeological grave contexts to include the social, historical and particular identity of the living person within his or her socio-religious community. Here we have a broad social portrait of well over one thousand individuals and mention of many of their associates who would, with rare exceptions, lie nameless in the grave otherwise. All this information alludes to both material and non-material aspects of burial, inherent in the definition of grave location and the placement of one's body there, from the perspective of the testator's own lived experience of familiar physical contexts. I will discuss the ramifications of the preceding statement at some length in Chapters 5 and 6.

In the next chapter, I take a look at how all the categories of information drawn from wills, pertaining to individual identity, grave location, and the use of material objects in association with the body, find expression in archaeological settings. Sometimes archaeological data complements the information contained within a will, but mostly it does not. I explore the content of archaeological site reports in relation to the content of the wills as described above, to better understand the disjunction between documentary and archaeological evidence when it comes to the interpretation of grave sites.

CHAPTER 3. WILLS AND SITE REPORTS AS SOURCES OF INFERENCE ABOUT GRAVE SITES

In what follows I examine the degree to which the content of the wills on testator's identity, grave location and requests for burial in some form of attire or piece of grave furniture is supplemented, supported or not represented in findings from various Spanish medieval church and cemetery sites. A related issue is the extent to which data derived from archaeological excavation approximates identity, location and recovery of action, as evidenced by survival of material objects, in individual terms in ways that are comparable, if not analogous to wills.

When we excavate a grave site, we are also unearthing more often than not the bones of one and sometimes several individuals. At some level, we share the testator's interest in being able to locate, identify and mark a grave site. This is the running theme that will recur throughout the remaining chapters of my book. Here, I use it to explore the tension between potential and actual recovery of data from the two sources, wills and site reports, at hand.

Criteria of Selection for Wills as Applied to Recovery of Material from Excavation of Grave Sites

It is possible to take either approach that I present below. Both are equally valid. My purpose in presenting them here is to provide a framework for subsequent discussion of specific information in the wills that is wholly or partially recovered in archaeological contexts and what is not.

An Inclusive Perspective

Any information from wills that touches on the location and disposition of a human body after death may have some bearing on interpretation of the physical evidence of bones, grave furnishings and graves unearthed in excavation. Broadly speaking, the data in my documentary sample have been selected because they refer to the identification of the testator's body - a tangible feature - in both spatial and temporal dimensions. From this point of view, not only the body but also the material context of the grave site itself, as well the specific social and historical circumstances of burial can all be manifested as tangible evidence. This is true - that is, what people attest in their wills we can take to be true - even if we do not have access to the physical remains of the people who left the wills, and even if the material, social and cultural contexts in which our testators lived, died and were buried no longer exist.

An Exclusive Perspective

At the same time, one could also argue that the salient aspects of information about bodies, graves and burials represented in the sample of wills, such as a testator's name, title, profession, parentage, family connections, and association with lay brotherhoods are not recoverable materially from excavation of grave sites. In addition the original contexts for burial have been destroyed. According to this logic, any data that describe the social identity of the testator and any statements about where, how, and why the body must be laid to rest in a certain spot cannot be counted as archaeological or recoverable information because they are not related to any actual physical evidence in our sites sample. I do not mean to say that archaeologists are unable to interpret the physical evidence of gravesites unless they have documents, such as wills, to which to refer. Though the specifics of the decision-making process evident in the wills are not visible or recoverable from the excavation of burials, we know that the physical evidence is the result of some structured human activity, repeated at irregular intervals at some time in the past.

I move on now from perspective to specifics. My order of presentation follows a trajectory from near convergence between the information found in wills and material counterparts found in excavation, to disjunction between the two data sets.

References in Wills to Material Objects Recovered from Excavation

References to material objects that might also be found in the excavation of a grave site are limited to what people asked to be buried in or buried with, and in a very few cases, how they wanted their graves to be marked or decorated. The range of variation among such requests is quite narrow; where burial attire is specified, the choice lies between a shroud, and a habit, with one or two exceptions. As to grave furniture, it is almost entirely restricted to mention of burial in coffins. Grave goods are scarcely mentioned in this sample. There are one or two cases of priests who specify inclusion of chalice and paten in their burials, as was customary (Rodwell 1989). In addition, a nobleman wishes his sword to be placed in his coffin;[1] and one woman asks that the scapular that she always carries be buried with her.[2]

Objects like those described in my sample of wills, or traces of them, have been documented in many different archaeological contexts. These contexts include not only Spanish and English church and cemetery sites of the late medieval period, but also historic period colonial sites in the New World, both Spanish and indigenous. In total the several sites that I shall refer to in this section span some five centuries, from the thirteenth through the late seventeenth centuries. Coverage is by no means equal or exhaustive and does not include mention of all sites recorded, or all site reports in my sample.

Overlaps between Wills and Site Reports

The use of shrouds has been inferred from shreds of linen fabric found at Valeria (Fernández Gonzalez 1981:111), or from the position of the feet, as at Tipu (Graham 1988:6). Coffin burials have been inferred by the recovery of wood as at Valdilecha (Bango Torviso 1981:119), but more usually because nails are positioned in the right places in association with the body as is the case in Tordesillas (García Tomás et. al. 1983:289). At both Valdilecha (1981:142) and Tordesillas (1983:287), use of a coffin is suggested by the recovery of pieces of metal that are situated where coffin handles would be. Pieces of braided leather recovered at Valdilecha are also thought to have been used as coffin handles (1981:142). Apart from chalices and patens found at Wharram Percy (Beresford and Hurst 1991:64) and a small wine jug (reserved for use in the liturgy), reported for Valdilecha (1981:140), there is no overlap between any particular item mentioned by a testator[3] and its appearance in an undisturbed grave context in any of the reports in my sample. Crosses and medals of the same period as the wills were also recovered at Valdilecha ((1981:142). What appear to be tombstones were discovered at Tiermes (Argente Oliver 1980:329-336) and San Juan de los Caballeros (Zamora Canellada 1979:590, 595). None of these are comparable to the markers and memorials that are noted by testators because of uncertainties in date, provenance, use and location.

Discrepancies between Wills and Site Reports

The only apparent discrepancy between data from the wills and data from site reports has to do with forms of burial attire. Religious habits become very popular items of burial attire in the course of the sixteenth and seventeenth centuries; as the wills attest, requests for burial in shrouds virtually disappear over the same period. No habit fragments are recorded for any of the excavated sites in my sample. On the other hand, there is a great deal of evidence from the late medieval site of Valeria (Fernández Gonzalez 1981) in the form of buckles, buttons, personal adornments and remains of leather and textiles

---

[1] Pedro Zapata de Cardenas, 1606, AHPM, Prot. 2015, fols. 1750r.-1758v.
... y a mi lado izquierdo mi espada dorada Ancha que yo traya en la guerra y es insignia del abito de mi Horden de Santiago... .
[2] Luisa de Peralta y Rebolledo, 1598, AHPM, Prot. 1810, fols. 1126r.-1131v. ...despues de aver fallecido el dicho mi cuerpo sea amortajado y me pongan el escapulario que yo traigo conmigo de la Santissima Trinidad... .
[3] Luis Nuñez, 1589, AHPM, Prot.186, unpaginated.
...una casulla comun y alba y manipulo y caliz de oja de lata y el demas recado que es costumbre y lo que costare se pague de mis bienes... .

to suggest that people were often dressed in their own clothing for burial. By way of contrast, only one testator in my sample of 1227 wills asks for burial in soldiers' dress, and to be wrapped in cloth of gold rather than in a regular habit or a shroud.[4]

This discrepancy may be a matter of "reading between the lines", or a question of what decays without leaving a trace and what doesn't, a shadow pattern with no significance beyond the vagaries of survival. Or it might reflect some change in custom that is meaningful in that it affected what people did, and what they thought worth mentioning. It brings us to the question of action in the wills and possible material manifestations of action in archaeological contexts.

Action in the Wills that is Suggested by the Recovery of Religious Attire in an Archaeological Context but which Cannot Be Confirmed by Archaeology Alone

There may be a whole range of reasons why a body discovered in excavation is clothed in the remains of a religious habit. A listing of reasons taken from my sample of wills would include: membership in a lay division of the order,[5] membership in the regular order[6] or wearing a habit because one is to be buried in a house of that same religious order.[7] Others include personal devotion to the founder of that religious order,[8] and a statement of the belief that indulgences will be gained by wearing a particular habit.[9] One man directs a plea for intercession on behalf of his soul to the saint whose habit he shall wear in death.[10] Some testators wish to be dressed for burial in a habit as death approaches, rather than afterwards.[11] Many others say nothing about why they choose a habit over a shroud other than that they view it as customary.[12]

In any case, even if we know about all these different motivations for wanting to be buried in a habit, when we are confronted with a grave in which the body has been so dressed, we are still left with the question of "why?" This is because there is no way to distinguish the particular reason for an individual decision, its subsequent manifestation as an action (putting a habit on a body), and the remains of a material object (the habit itself) from either the wills or the excavation itself. On the other hand, the wills have at least told us to expect reasons in a particular range, and have also told us it is a matter of personal choice.

Action in the Wills Linked to Material that may be Recovered in an Archaeological Context but Not Suggested by the Material Itself: The Example of Masses

Many actions leave no material manifestation that would be recoverable archaeologically, even when they are closely tied in with material objects or spaces that archaeologists would be able to define in excavation. We may know from reading a testator's will that she wanted her body to be disinterred after a period of time and moved to another parish or that she asked for masses to be sung over her grave in the hope of a sure passage from Purgatory to Heaven. We might also learn how many masses the testator wanted, how these might be named and numbered in dedication to some aspect of Christ or the Virgin

---

[4] Luis de Cordoba y Aragon, 1596, AHPM, Prot. 1808, fols. 759r.-760v.
...y que me entierren en abito de soldado en el vestido de tela de oro que tengo en mi baul... .
[5] Alonso de Luzon, 1613, AHPM, Prot. 2012, fols. 280r.-289v.
...en avito de la tercera orden de San Francisco y encima del me pongan el manto del capitulo de la orden de Santiago donde soy profeso... .
[6] Mariana Lopez de Ayllon, 1603, AHPM, Prot. 2009, fols. 759r.-764v.
...metido en abito del bienadventurado San Anton mi abogado de cuya horden soy hermana... .
[7] Juana de Rojas, 1564, AHPM, Prot. 314, fols. 518r.-519r.
...en abito de San Francisco de Paula que es orden del dicho monesterio [de Nuestra Señora de la Victoria]... .
[8] Geronima de Acosta, 1602, AHPM, Prot. 1427, unpaginated.
...me entierren con el avito de Nra Sra del Carmen con el qual quiero morir por la gran devocion que tengo con su orden... .
[9] Paula de Castelvi, 1625, AHPM, Prot. 4021, fols. 695r.-698r.
...que mi cuerpo sea enterrado con el abito de Nra. Sra. del Carmen ... y por su divina magestad sea en vida de que yo goce de sus yndulgencias... .
[10] Gabriel de Cardenas, 1611, AHPM, Prot. 2009, fols. 1122r.-1126v.
...en abito del serafico San Francisco mi abogado a quien suplico interceda por mi con Nuestro Señor Jesu Cristo... .
[11] Alonso Montalban, 1577, AHPM, Prot. 778, fols. 545r.-549v.
...el dia de mi muerte antes que salga el anima de mi cuerpo me sea puesto el avito del Sr San Francisco para que muriera en el... .
[12] Alonso de Toledo, 1530, AHPM, Prot. 55, fols. 875r.-876v.
...en el abito de San Pedro como es uso en esta villa... .

Mary, or in honor of saints, apostles, martyrs, angels, and even legendary figures.[13] A testator who emphasized masses would certainly detail when (during funeral ceremonies and after burial), where (masses could be allocated to different graves, altars, or chapels, in churches other than the place where the testator is buried) and at what intervals or anniversaries masses might be given in his memory, or in memory of family members and other associates (Eire 1995).

The decision to have mass said over one's body in the grave is not an insignificant one because it involves earthly expense, but more important, it might make the difference, from a personal point of view, between the life or death of the soul for all Eternity. For us it is an important example of a significant decision, an action contingent on burial location no less, that leaves absolutely no trace in archaeological excavation.

Location: When Material Patterning is supported by Documentary Data but Disjunction Remains

The distinction between actual and potential recovery of data can be best illustrated by discussion of the sequence of "identifiers" that testators use in the wills to indicate where they want to be buried. Such identifiers at a minimum include mention of the city in which the will was drawn up, parish affiliation, the building in which the grave plot was to be located, and the avocation of both parish and place of burial. Insofar as this sequence describes what an archaeologist would call "burial location," the archival data do appear to support our understanding of material patterning of gravesites in archaeological terms. On the other hand the information on burial location is often not defined in ways that facilitate location by excavation. In this respect, the most archaeological question of all - locational context - cannot be recovered directly from the documentary sources available to us. This disjunction will be explored in considerable detail in succeeding chapters of the present work.

The testator's place of burial is sometimes denoted by mention of the name of a parish, which may or may not correspond to the church where the grave is actually located. There is no necessary connection between the physical structure that is a church and its designation as a parish. The parish is a social construct that is meaningful to people when associated with a particular church. Even if the name of the parish itself were emblazoned on a building under excavation, we could not know what it signified unless we retained a historical awareness of what a parish is.

Another dimension of space is provided by references to the location of the grave within a particular architectural environment such as a church, monastery, or hospital. One or two or three or more of these categories tell us where or in what location the testator wanted his or her grave to be marked, opened, or newly dug, but personal and social reasons for choosing one location over another are not apparent in the archaeological context. The dedication of a church, monastery or hospital to a particular saint is what differentiates it from another building of the same genre, no matter how similar in date and construction, as we will see on closer analysis of texts in later chapters.

In a few instances, the city or town where the person drew up the will is not the place of death or even of final burial, and in these cases bodies are often moved from an expedient to a permanent location. The fact of secondary burial is detectable archaeologically but the meaning attached to such a move is a socio-historical construct and not recoverable through excavation.

---

[13] Menzia Salzedo, 1552, AHPM, Prot. 147, fols. 831r.-839r.
...desde el dia que mi cuerpo sea sepoltado en un mes se digan por mi anima las misas siguientes: ...tres misas de la Santissima Trinidad, padre, hijo e espiritu santo; siete misas de la encarnacion del hijo de Dios en testimonio que bajo el hijo de Dios por su encarnacion y passion redimio el linage humano y en la confianca que sere yo uno de los redimidos;...cinco misas de la cruz, y en las quattro dellas se digan las quattro passiones y en la quinta el evangelio propio de la misa de la cruz, porque Jhu Xpo nuestro senor por su muerte y ressureccion me de la vida eterna en su sancta gloria;...siete misas del Espiritu Sancto en testimonio de la confianca que tengo firme que por sus sanctos siete dones estara mi anima dispuesta para salir deste mundo y gozar de su reino celestial;...las nueve misas de nuestra senora la Virgen Madre de Dios conviene a saber la concepcion de nra sra, el nascimiento de nra senora, la encarnacion del hijo de Dios, el nascimiento, purificacion, visitacion, la fiesta de las nieves, spetacio partus, la asuncion por la especial y gran devocion y confianca que yo tengo y siempre he tenido en esta soberana Virgen que por su amparo e yntercesion alcanzara la salvacion de mi anima... .

In other instances testators identify the spot within the general locale of a church or monastery where their bodies are to be laid in specific terms by reference to a series of markers, which convey a relative sense of the placement of the body at best. A testator might ask to be buried in an area of the church building, such as a chapel or nave entrance that is meaningfully distinguished, although it may not always be physically separated or visibly marked. Where various means of access to a grave-plot are recorded, we know that the body is destined for a particular spot, but we may not know where on the ground. I shall elaborate on all these points with the support of particular examples in Chapter 4.

The documents may reveal that a body is directed to be buried near, next to, or in the same plot as the body or bodies of kinfolk or those of some other group, such as monks, nuns, friars, brothers in a lay confraternity or brothers of the third order of Saint Francis. No matter how specific these markers look on paper, the majority would not be identifiably linked to their original context on the strength of excavation method alone, because much of their meaning is external to a strictly archaeological context.

Identity: Archaeologically Recovered Data that has No Counterpart in the Wills at All

There are several pieces of information that are important to archaeological understanding of grave sites and the identification of the dead which do not form any part of wills. These include age of the deceased and the position of the body in the grave, as well as the head orientation.

Age

In the wills there is never any mention of the age of the testator. In one or two instances there are references that suggest that a person may be relatively old, as when the graves of grandchildren are mentioned,[14] or young, as when a person leaves his or her parents to arrange the details of coffin furniture.[15] Juan de la Ripia provides a nearly contemporary reference to the question of who is old enough to leave a will. In a work entitled, Practica de Testamentos y Modos de Subceder, he declares that "women may make wills at age twelve or older and boys starting at age fourteen, regardless of whether they are still in their parents charge" (de la Ripia 1674:25).

The important thing to note about minimum ages of testators is that people who do not leave wills, including children and the poor or dispossessed are not represented. Any possible information about preparation of the body for burial, the use of distinctive attire, or otherwise special treatment in accordance with social standing is lost. It might be found in other kinds of documents that list funeral costs or in confraternity records or even parish registers, but I was not able to encompass any of these in my archival research. This is unfortunate from an archaeological point of view, because there is some evidence from Tipu, for example, which suggests that children, more than adults, were buried with European goods (Graham 1989:8).

Yet in many excavations, a person's age at death, if it can be judged by what remains, is often taken to be a significant factor in interpreting possible distribution patterns. At several sites in my sample, the relative proportions of adult to infant or pre-adult bodies are noted on the basis of skeletal remains, as at L'Esquerda (Ollich i Castanyer 1982:127), or measurement of grave dimensions as at the sites of Agreda (de la Casa Martinez 1985:281) and Hoyos de los Peñones (Puertas Tricas 1982:285). Sometimes the recording of relative distribution of remains by age is used as an indicator for the demographic representation and density of remains that would be uncovered at the site, if it were to be completely excavated, as at San Juan de los Caballeros (Zamora Canellada 1979). Only rarely at these sites is there any overt suggestion that a person's age at death might have something to do with the relative location of their burial such that these two factors combined represent a pattern that has some intrinsic meaning. The pattern could be burial with other family members, as at Las Mesas de Villaverde (Ramos

---

[14] Anton Sanchez, 1562, AHPM, Prot. 313, fols. 586r.-587r.
...debaxo de la tribuna de los organos en la sepultura de una nieta mia... .
[15] Luis de Cordoba y Aragon, loc. cit.
...Y ruego a mis padres que pongan una plancha de cobre... .

Fernández 1979:169). Or it might refer to burial in a specific locale according to a particular age cohort as is suggested in the site reports for San Lorenzo (Delgado Valero 1988: 363) and San Miguel de Escalada (Larren Izquierdo 1989:120).

The infant bodies found buried under household doorways dating from the tenth, possibly thirteenth, and as late as the early fifteenth centuries (Riu 1982:191), - this last reported in a sealed deposit under the floor of an interior room - are exceptional in my sites sample. In all cases, a medieval bishop's report is cited as an explanation for these finds. It alludes to the widespread belief among practicing Christians that burial of a baptized infant at the threshold of a house served to protect its occupants from evil (Riu 1982:199). These finds are important additions to our knowledge of burial practices and associations among medieval Spanish Christians derived from excavation. Archival research followed, rather than preceded, discovery of the bodies as with most of the other sites in this sample. Such an expanded range of possibilities finds no counterpart in the wills.

Body Position

The position of the body as it is originally laid in the grave upon burial is information that by and large is not recoverable from this sample of wills. Body position may be pre-figured in two cases where the testator describes the way that she is to be laid out when death approaches,[16] and during the funeral ceremonies at the church, prior to burial.[17] Such details are echoed in accounts of the death agonies of the Hapsburg kings, and may well have been inspired by their example (Orso 1989; Varela 1990).

In some of the Spanish sites in my sample, bodies which are not found in an extended supine position with arms folded across the chest or abdomen are interpreted as evidence of a non-Christian tradition of burial practice. Laying the body on its right side, with the head facing south or east, as at La Torrecilla (Riu 1974) and San Nicolas de Murcia (Navarro Palazon 1989:8), is indisputable evidence of Islamic burial practices as all Muslims were buried facing Mecca. At any site where Jewish burials are historically documented, as at Montjuich in Barcelona (Duran Sanpere and Millas à 1947:233) or late medieval urban cemetery sites such as El Circo Romano just outside the city of Toledo (Juan Garcia 1989:647), where Christian, Muslim and Jewish burials may overlap, body position in itself is not enough to identify distinctive traditions of burial.

Such identification depends on association through archaeological or historical work with various levels of church construction as is the case at San Miguel de Escalada (Larren Izquierdo: 1989) and at Tiermes (Argente Oliver 1980). Sometimes it may depend on general historical knowledge of populations and patterns of re-settlement in the area, as for example at Biota (Labe Valenzuela 1985), or on comparative typologies of grave goods or grave construction, as is noted at Montjuich (Duran Sanpere and Millas Vallicrosa 1947:244). At least one site, that of La Lampara (Fernandez Nanclares et. al. 1985:402), is identified as Christian on the basis of a combination of expectations and guesswork.

---

[16] Menzia Salzedo, 1552, AHPM, Prot. 147, fols. 831r.-839r.
...la candela que yo tuviere en la mano al tiempo de mi fallescimiento en testimonio de la luz de la fe catolica con que mi anima entonces estara alumbrada, se guarde para que se lleve en mi enterramiento y se ponga sobre mi sepultura en quanto se hiziere el officio de difuntos, ansimismo una cruz con figura de Xpo crucificado que yo deseo y espero tener en la otra mano a la ora de mi fallescimiento en manifestacion de la fe y esperanza que yo tengo de aquel maravillosisimo misterio, y de ser por el salvar mi anima... .
[17] Maria de Arnalte y Palomino, 1602, AHPM, Prot. 1427, fols.779r.-788r.
...luego que yo sea fallescida y passada de esta presente vida a la otra, se pongan dos cirios de cera que alumbren bien mi cuerpo y encima del me pongan un crucifijo y que desta manera retengan sin me enterrar hasta que ayan passado veynte quatro oras de como yo fallesciere, Al cabo de las quales me lleven a enterrar con el avito del senor San Francisco en el qual procuro morir para ganar las indulgencias y perdones que les estan concedidas... .

Head Orientation

Regarding head orientation, there is nothing in my sample of wills on the subject, because it was something for the gravedigger rather than the testator to decide. Preferred head/grave orientation in alignment with the west/east axis of all medieval Christian churches, so that the main entrance to the church is on the west side of the building and the altar is located inside at the east end, opposite the west door, is documented in many early sources (Durandus 1893). Medieval Spain presents no exception to this rule as both archaeological finds and historical sources attest. Where bodies have been unearthed in numbers from church cemeteries, at Valeria, Agreda, Tiermes and San Juan de los Caballeros, to cite some examples that we have used so far, grave and head orientation has conformed to this pattern in that bodies are interred with heads to the west and feet to the east. For Madrid in particular, I could not locate any references to documented archaeological excavations of any of the churches mentioned in the wills.

On the subject of church orientation however, we have the word of Geronimo de Quintana, author of a work first published in 1629, entitled A la Muy Antigua, Noble y Coronada Villa de Madrid, Historia de su Antiguedad, Nobleza y Grandeza. He says: " all [the parochial churches in Madrid] have the high altar to the east (except for that in the church of San Juan which faces to the south and that of San Martin which is to the west), according to the ancient custom of the church, which stems from the time of the Apostles...". Quintana goes on to note that in the present time, church orientation is no longer governed by this custom, venerable and true as it may be: "...nowadays, when a church is founded, one does not look to the propriety of the situation of the high altar, so much as to the fit, disposition and capacity of the site where the work is to be carried out."[18] That the medieval rule of thumb on building orientation does not hold for every church built or refurbished after the Counter-Reformation, is further borne out by archaeological excavation at the church site of Bergus. Here the original orientation of the church was completely altered in the seventeenth century by re-building the ruined apse where the principal entrance had once been (Bertrán Roigé 1982:177).

In summary, the assumption that head orientation, if it is in alignment with a building that is demonstrably a church of Christian worship, is a diagnostic for Christian burial practice, appears to be supported by the testimony presented above. By the same token, it is clear that a consistent church orientation may not always be observed, for reasons which may have nothing to do with the belief systems which support a particular pattern of alignment.

Defining the Disjunction between Data Sets: Burial and Grave Site

So far I have chronicled the path of divergence between information contained in wills and material that is or can be recovered from archaeological excavation. Perhaps the best way to describe the lack of fit between the two sets of data is to examine the nuances of "burial" and "grave site."

---

[18] de Quintana, Geronimo. 1629. A la Muy Antigua, Noble y Coronada Villa de Madrid. Historia de su Antiguedad, Nobleza y Grandeza. ed. facs. 1980. José Ramon Aguado. Madrid: Abaco Ediciones.

Todas [las iglesias parroquiales de Madrid] tienen el altar mayor al oriente (sino es la de San Juan que la tiene al Septentrion, y la de San Martin al Occidente) segun la costumbre antigua de la yglesia, emanada desde el tiempo de los Apostoles, de quien dijo Zacharias: Estaran los pies del Señor en el Oriente, para que como dize el Profeta Rey: Adoremos al Señor en el lugar donde estuvieron los pies. Otra razon da San Anastasio por estas palabras: Oygan los fieles, y sepan la causa por que los Santos Apostoles mandoron hazer las Iglesias de los Christianos hazia el Oriente, donde hiziessen oracion: porque mirando al parayso de donde fuimos echados, pidamos humilmente a Dios nuestro Señor que nos quiera restituyr y bover a aquella antigua patria y lugar de donde caimos. Lo qual no arguye pequeña antiguedad, por ser costumbre emanada del tiempo de los Apostoles, como dize Atanasio: principalmente que en este quando se funda un templo, no se mira tanto a la propiedad de la situacion del Altar mayor, quanto a la comodidad, disposion y capacidad del sitio en que se ha de hazer la obra.

Burial in Wills

"Burial" has much broader implications than "grave site". In the context of the wills I use it to denote a whole complex of practices and beliefs mentioned by testators that refer to preparation of the body for burial, as well as the act of burial itself. This encompasses the death of the testator as a physical event and as part of the social process. All information in the archival data is pertinent to our understanding of burial, from the social identity of the testator, including his or her sex, name, marital status, profession etc., through what might be called a "socio-religious network". Mention of spouse by name, place of origin, mention of parents' origin, mention of other relatives, and choice of grave location may be indicative of such a network, at the very least. It might also extend to mention of particular devotions, attachments or associations with particular confraternities, saints, and their shrines or churches through requests for habits, accompaniment, funeral masses, mourning attire, and the expressed desire to be buried and/or memorialized with a tomb in proximity to any one or more of these. A burial thus defined is an inference, rather than a fact in archaeological terms.

Graves in Archaeology

A grave site in both documentary and archaeological contexts is exactly that: the spot where the grave is dug and the body interred. In archaeological reports there is often more than one way to describe and locate this spot. Location may be expressed in relation to an arbitrary, fixed point on a grid, or in terms of vertical stratigraphy, or by marking the position of abrupt changes in coloration of soil (McIntosh 1986). These changes could be indicators in various instances of grave outlines, skeletal remains, grave furniture, or grave markers (Rodwell 1989), depending upon soil conditions and the length of time that the site has been used as a burial ground. Graves and any bodies that still remain in them may be numbered and referenced according to excavation sequence as at L'Esquerda (Ollich i Castanyer 1982), which in turn may have a lot to do with the positioning of one burial in relation to another, especially in areas with high burial densities, such as the south exterior walls of a church, as opposed to a low frequency of burials on the north side as at Tipu (Graham and Bennett 1989:3) or none at all in that quarter, as is the case at Agreda (de la Casa Martinez 1985:247). The location of grave sites is also marked chronologically in many medieval Christian contexts in terms of possible associations with the definition of various phases of church construction, where the excavation is large enough in scope as at San Juan de los Caballeros (Zamora Canellada 1979:597). Last but not least, location can be illustrated with contour maps, grid maps, stratigraphic profiles, picture maps, scale drawings and photography.

The Connotation of Grave Site in Archaeology and in the Wills

From all this we may conclude, rightly, that "grave site" carries a precise connotation in archaeology. It can be pinpointed on the ground. Consequently, we can claim that its existence is documented fact rather than inference, even if we only have a report to go by, because it is contained in material terms that are potentially identifiable in many excavations.

By the same token, "grave site" in the context of the wills, though it may be used to indicate that every testator in the sample must have ended up in one, is not entirely interchangeable with the grave site of archaeological reports. As will be seen in the next chapter, the wording that testators use to describe where they want to be buried is precise and to the point for their purpose. They rely on their contemporaries' knowledge of physical setting and social ties to fill in the blanks; but this of course does not do for us, for we lack knowledge, memory and full record of those contexts. If all specific mention of markers - whether these are plots containing the bodies of deceased relatives, tombstones, holy images, architectural features, or liturgically defined sacred spaces within a church, or a combination of some of the above - were somehow mapped onto a hypothetical amalgamation of all buildings in the sample, this huge effort would not confirm our understanding of exactly where a testator's grave site and his or her body would have been buried in the same way that we understand grave site in an archaeological context. In this regard burial location in the wills is a matter of inference because it is not materially identifiable with the location of graves and bodies in an excavation.

What Happens Next: Shifting Disjunction from Data to Perspective

All that has been said above indicates a disjunction between material manifestation of grave location (in physical setting) and identity (in body) as indicated in the wills and archaeological recovery of the same. Data derived from archaeological excavation do not approximate identity, location and recovery of action, as evidenced by survival of material objects, in individual terms in ways that are comparable to wills. This is to be expected.

Grave location as it is defined within a will is partly congruent with what might be described in an archaeological context. Some categories of reference denote physical spaces or features on a scale that is small enough to be recognized at individual sites.

Neither content nor criteria for defining individual identity are congruent between wills and site reports as we have seen. The only link that may be drawn between testators and archaeologists from what has been said so far is that both are talking about bodies, individuals, people in graves. It is an important link, for both refer directly or indirectly, to action. Archaeologists tend to see action only in terms of surviving material outcomes. Testators present us with an opportunity to observe live action in a prospective context.

Much more will be said in later chapters on this topic, but I mention it now because we cannot reconcile the data on identity and location from wills with excavated grave sites on the basis of material evidence alone. The end result can only be the flat and somewhat arbitrary distinction made above between burial and grave site.

We must articulate the individual in the grave through another set of parameters, through an exploration of both our own and testator's perspectives on grave location and through a study of their action and identity as expressed in their own words. Only then can we begin to understand how the material remains that we see in excavation of a grave site fit together with all that we do not see, but once was there.

CHAPTER 4. RECOGNITION AND REPRESENTATION OF GRAVE LOCATION FROM THE PERSPECTIVES OF ARCHAEOLOGIST AND TESTATOR

In this chapter I am presenting a different perspective on the concept of location as a result of my familiarity with what testators have said in their wills about their own burials. Location encompasses the expectation of executors, family, friends and others arriving at the grave site where the testator's body lies. My view takes into account archaeologists' concepts of location as well as the ways in which people pinpoint objects or landmarks (such as graves) in living contexts such as those contexts depicted in the wills. The various examples that I discuss below may then lead to a greater appreciation of the interpretive possibilities inherent in any perspectives on location.

I proceed on the conviction that location is not a given, but a construct. It is an object of thought constituted by the ordering or systematic uniting of experiential elements as precepts and sense data, and of terms and relations. A construct of location is made up of a combination of what I (or you or someone else) see in space (what is visible and tangible to me and others) and what I think I need to see (how I create that which is visible and tangible in my mind's eye) in order to arrive at that location. In this scheme of things, my perception of a given space or location directs my search almost as much as the external indicators of that location do.

Archaeological Criteria of Location: Terms of Recognition

Some archaeological criteria of location are susceptible to recognition; others are a factor in representation. We may think of recognition as an identity already known: a form of memory consistent with previous experience of a thing or person. As such, recognition of a location within an archaeological context is rooted in perceptions of objects and spaces that are likely to be consistent with the perceptions of other archaeologists who view them. There are three criteria of location that fit the terms of recognition.

Recognition is All in A Name: Location is Identified in order to be Accounted for

All locational markers can be identified or accounted for by being named. By way of example, a piece of rock may be discovered in conjunction with a hole in the ground containing human bones. If there is some reason to believe that the hole was dug deliberately to receive the body and that this same rock was laid there to commemorate the dead, than we identify that hole as a grave and designate that rock a grave stone.

Recognition is rooted in the Material World: Sight and Touch Define Location

Recognition is also premised on the notion that all locational markers correspond to some material object, or some space that is defined in a physical context, or to sub-surface excavation of skeletal remains. In the present context, locational markers correspond to such objects as altar and choir grilles, chapel walls and entryways, altars, stoups, windows, doors, steps, floor tiles, pillars, gravestones, sculptured monuments, carved images, retables, pulpits, confessionals, graves, and crosses. Chapel interiors, burial vaults, altar niches, sacristy, nave and choir, cloister, garden and outdoor cemetery, all are spaces defined within the physical contexts of the parish, monastery and hospital churches named in the wills. Locational markers also correspond to skeletal remains, in a hypothetical sense at least, with every request for burial in or near the grave of a loved one or in the tomb or vault of a friend, acquaintance, patron, ancestor or distant family connection.

Recognition is Premised on Ordered Relations: All Locations and Spaces are Susceptible to Measurement

Finally, a third criterion of archaeological location that is amenable to recognition in the sense defined above is that all physical objects and corporeal bodies are located by measuring the interval of space between them and their distance from an arbitrary "datum" point. This point may be set up outside the confines of the spatial context under study (Rodwell 1989). The system of notation used to express points in space, be they bones, graves, tomb monuments, altars or chapels etcetera, is numerical (Rodwell 1989) and bears no relation to the essence of the object or space itself. Two implications of the preceding statement must be spelled out here.

The ordering of such points in space is primarily derived from recording the chronological sequence of recovery from excavation contexts. We locate a set of bones by assigning a number to them. The number defines them as a point of reference. It does not identify them, even though we know that skeletal remains correspond to the bodies of people who once existed.

Spaces between points are not adequately described by numbers. The numbers assigned to skeletal remains also place them in a stratigraphy that expresses the depth and order in which excavation was carried out. They are inserted into a system of relations in space that assigns no value to the positions in space that are not presently or visibly (at the moment of recovery) occupied by human bones. Objects of another kind or spaces that intrude into this sequence are given a sequence of their own or are simply not represented within the system.

In consequence, observed spaces can only be integrated by accumulating a series of maps of points of location of different classes of objects that may bear no actual relation to each other, apart from the fact of recording them in a chronological order reversed from that of excavation (Rodwell 1989). I will carry the point no further except to say that the ways in which we have been trained to see and set down our perceptions of association, correspondence and relation of objects and bodies in space weigh heavily on how we represent archaeological criteria of location.

Archaeological Criteria of Location: Terms of Representation

We may think of representation here as an idea that is a mental counterpart or transcript of the object known by means of it. It is not based on a form of memory, as is recognition. Rather, it draws on associations or expectations that we form around the attributes or nature of the idea, in this case location that is the object of thought. It is a mental image born of a particular orientation towards a specific experience of a particular space, here of a hypothetical excavation of a church that may or may not be reinforced by one's training. Unlike recognition, representation is not always manifest in a material sense. Representation of location as that location is actually defined within an archaeological context is subject to greater variation than recognition of the same. Here I present six criteria of location that fit the terms of representation for archaeological excavation of gravesites in church and cemetery contexts.

Representation of Points in Space: All Locations are Discrete

All locations, i.e. points or positions filled in space, are represented as being discrete from one another. Somehow it is expected that all locations are clearly demarcated or separate from each other. This representation (locations are discrete) works only when location is defined on the basis of skeletal remains, grave pits or some other kind of distinctive artifact or object present in the ground. It does not work when location is expressed in terms of blocks of space unless the intervals between one point or more and another point in space are also articulated by some numeric measurement.

Representation of Points in Space: All Locations are Isolates

Location may also be represented as an isolate. The object, body or space that fills a given spot is expected to translate easily into a single point that falls into a precise set of coordinates somewhere on an imaginary gridline. In this representation, X literally marks the spot. If a object, body or space is related to other objects, bodies or spaces in an ordered sequence as in the example of the stratigraphy of skeletal remains discussed earlier, it may still be singled out from that sequence as an isolate in terms of location because no other of its kind can occupy that point in space without altering the entire sequence.

Representation of Points in Space: All Locations are Fixed in Time and Space

A third representation of location involves the idea that a given point in space, be it a church, a grave, a chapel, pillar, a wall, a set of stairs, anything that we choose to focus our attention on, is expected to be fixed in time as well as space. The expectation that a family will continue the practice of burial of all family members of all succeeding generations in their own private chapel, without exception or interruption, or that all family tombs in the chapel will survive intact through the ages are examples of "fixed" representations of location in time and space respectively. Archaeologists and testators alike may find it more comfortable to assume that graves (especially their own in the case of testators) are somehow permanent, or at least not likely to be removed from the space they occupy for a very long time. Both historical and archaeological records demonstrate the flaws in such an assumption.

Representation of Points in Space: All Locations are Expressible as Compass Directions

A fourth representation of location stems from the assumption that all positions in space are properly expressed as compass directions. Issues of recognition and representation are at work here. In the language of the compass, space is partitioned on a grid-form, a universal template that is recognized intuitively by everyone without translation. The four-part template may be applied to any surface whether we ourselves create that surface or merely perceive one created by someone else. This is not to say that the representation of location as a point on a compass is applied to every space and surface those men have created. It is not. I illustrate the apparent paradox with the following examples.

When we use north, south, east and west to describe the alignment of graves that we have uncovered in excavation, we are in effect recording a leveled plane, a surface that we have created in pursuit of an ordered view. This surface is not equivalent to the burial ground that a person would recognize and expect to be interred in, despite the fact that a predictable pattern of grave alignment based on what we perceive to be compass directions is followed at cemeteries associated with churches, with only occasional and specific deviations from the norm (Rodwell 1989). Compass directions are not likely to be represented in the mind of a person who is deciding upon the criteria for location of his or her grave, because there is no need to do so. Personal concerns, such as where the family plot is, or how much it costs to buy or open a grave, will predominate in his or her thoughts, judging by the evidence. It is left to the executors, and ultimately the gravedigger, to take care of the details between them.

When we say that a church is aligned on an east-west axis and the principal doorway is located at the west end of the building, we are seeing a surface, excavated or not, that has been created on a grid plan. Indications of an understanding of space that is analogous to the divisions of the compass do exist in the wills. When a testator asks for a grave at the foot of the church it is quite likely that he or she is referring to the west end of the building (Bottomley 1978). Again, despite a well-documented association, we cannot claim that location is actually represented here in the language of the compass, despite a parallel understanding of location on a quadripartite body axis. In short there is a gap here between recognition of space and our way of representing it that will be explored below in greater detail.

Representation of Points in Space: All Locations Correspond to "Filled" Spaces

Finally, location may be represented in two ways that complement each other and may hark back to the numeric bias inherent in our expectation that all locations and spaces are susceptible to measurement. The first of these representations involves the idea that there exists a one on one correspondence between the object or body or space that takes up any given location and the location itself. In other words, location is seen to be filled up by one material object or body of a particular kind. A point in space can consist of only one primary material element at any given time. It is much easier to indicate location by specifying only one kind of marker at a given spot, even if more than one is in evidence at that same site and clearly associated with the other(s).

By way of a hypothetical example, ninety-nine positions in space may be taken up by un-coffined bodies placed in rectangular pits. Four more pits are lined with stones, three contain coffins, and one of the pits containing a coffin is also topped at ground level by a stone lid. The multiplicity of locational markers and disparate frequency of associations render a single comprehensive sequence of points in space that correspond to only one material object or body of a particular kind, or one primary material element at any given time, a complete impossibility. Along the same line of thought, more than one of anything is always worthy of remark. When more than one set of bones is discovered in what looks to be a single grave, it is always a matter of note (Rodwell 1989), perhaps because it disrupts the regularity of an ordered sequence.

Representation of Points in Space: All Locations that Correspond to the same kind of "Filled Space" are Considered Equivalent to Each Other

The corollary representation of location stems from the notion that a single object, body, or space of a particular type does not necessarily have to be taken into consideration as a singular example belonging to a larger, more general class of similar things, but simply an example equivalent to every other object, body or space of its type. According to this logic, one grave stone is much the same as another, simply because it shares certain features with other objects that we identify as grave stones on the basis of positioning and function, regardless of what variation in form and content may tell us.

Testing Archaeological Criteria of Location: Challenges to the Terms of Recognition Drawn from Examples in the Wills

The wills provide us with an opportunity to test our criteria of recognition and representation with reference to descriptions of location that are meant to direct people so that they arrive at a specific destination. In all cases the testator's grave is that destination. There is only one right location if we look at it this way.

In examining the wills for references to location then, we are actually juggling two expectations as to what will be found in them. One is that archaeological criteria of recognition and representation, as outlined in the preceding section, will be met. The other is that any reference to these criteria in a statement of location will be sufficient to allow us to "find" that grave, were we to apply that description of location to a hypothetical setting of a church.

A close study of the documentary evidence violates both expectations. The next several sections of the present chapter are devoted to a presentation of particular examples of statements of grave location to illustrate the ways in which our expectations are not borne out by the specific content of various texts.

Markers are Not Always Identified as Belonging to A Particular Class of Object

Mariana de la Cruz asks for a grave "however it may be, as close as possible to the Most Holy Sacrament".[1] Geronima Montoya wishes to be buried "in front of Our Lady of Peace".[2] In both examples a physical marker associated with the preferred location of burial is named, but the nature of the object is not further specified. We may assume that the Most Holy Sacrament and Our Lady of Peace refer to the Host and an image of some sort. We may further infer that both are associated with altars, as we know from experience that such objects usually are. It is also possible that altars or chapels are the true points of reference being named here. In the absence of any other qualifying statement we cannot claim to know what the Most Holy Sacrament and Our Lady of Peace are, nor where they are. In consequence, we cannot specify grave location on the basis of the markers that are given in either of these examples. In an archaeological frame of reference they do not mark anything at all, because they cannot be identified with particular objects.

Space is Often Characterized on a Non-Material Plane

Descriptions of location that refer to associations rather than physical characteristics of a space or objects within that space provide us with examples of spaces that are characterized on a non-material plane. Luis de Toledo y Mendoza wishes to be buried "inside the nun's choir of which I am patron".[3] Here we are presented with two non-material associations. The grave is located in a space that is distinguished by association with the people who use it and by the testator's personal claim as patron of that space. As such it is differentiated from any other choir that does not share in those associations.

No Order of Relations is Suggested and No Measurement in Space is Possible When Location is Given as Being Synonymous with the Grave Itself

Diego de Buitrago, like many others in my sample of wills, simply designates location by saying "in the grave that we have there".[4] This is the ultimate statement of location that we seek, but in a practical context, the information that a grave exists in space is not sufficient to help us find it. No order of relations is suggested and no measurement in space is possible. In short, my expectation that location is adequately expressed in a statement that parallels a numerical notation of a point in space is not confirmed.

Testing Archaeological Criteria of Location: Challenges to the Terms of Representation Drawn from Examples in the Wills

Material Elements Are Not Always Discrete Even When They Differ

Juana Lopez says that she wants to be buried "inside the church in a place with a window".[5] Here a material element, the window, is incorporated into the wall of the church. As such it is not perceived as being physically discrete from the building itself, even though it is produced as a separate object and is usually made from glass, a material not found in the walls. A section of wall that is taken up with a window is not necessarily considered to be discontinuous in space from a section of wall that lacks a window. Locating a grave to fit the description of "a place with a window" suggests a distinctive combination of material elements (window and wall) that differ from one another and so serve to mark

---

[1] Mariana de la Cruz, 1613, AHPM, Prot. 2012, fols. 1176r.-1179r.
...como sea lo mas cerca possible al Santissimo Sacramento... .
[2] Geronima Montoya, 1589, AHPM, Prot. 1800, fols. 444r.-447r.
...enfrente de Nuestra Señora de la Paz...
[3] Luis de Toledo y Mendoza, 1598, AHPM, Prot. 1810, fols. 194r.-198r.
...dentro del coro de las monjas donde yo soy patron... .
[4] Diego de Buitrago, 1580, AHPM, Prot. 775, fols. 794r.-797v.
...en la sepultura que alli tenemos... .
[5] Juana Lopez, 1507, AHPM, Prot. 19, unpaginated.
...en la yglesia en un lugar con ventana... .

the desired spot. It does not render that window, wall and grave a place separate from the surrounding space in the perception of all who encounter it, unless some physical barrier were to be constructed against the wall around that grave or the grave was marked out in some other way.

Objects and Designated Spaces are Not Isolates

Magdalena de Reinoso asks for a grave "right up next to the Holy Water stoup which is at the door of the church".[6] Both the stoup and the doorway are integral to an understanding of where the grave is to be laid, so much so that neither can be subtracted from her statement without prejudice to our understanding of location. From the point of view of meaning they are not isolates. If we consider them in terms of the practical effect of locating the grave itself, they cannot be considered without relation to one another. "Next to the Holy Water stoup" is the primary designate of location, but it is the aggregation of "which is next to the door of the church" that really gives us an orientation in the space that is indicated by mention of the former.

Some "Fixed Elements" may be removed to Some Other Place at Any Time

Catalina Gomez requests "a grave next to the grille of the High Altar which is now in the said church, or wherever the said Altar may be made when I should die".[7] We tend to expect that High Altars are somehow fixed in place by both convention and construction, but the above statement indicates that such an expectation is not always justified. Altars, like the churches in which they are housed or like any other item in continuous use over many years, are subject to removal, repair and refurbishment, without restoration to their former appearance or relative placement in their original surroundings. Obviously, this occurred often enough for Catalina Gomez to take it into account in describing the whereabouts of her intended grave site.

Directions are Indicated Via Use of, or Movement Though Space and Not by Compass

Francisco de Vera asks for "the grave that is in the choir next to the gospel [side of the altar] as people enter [the choir], where my mother is buried".[8] The reader of his will is directed to his grave by a reference to the path that would be taken to enter the choir. A second reference is provided via mention of the Gospel side of the altar. Convention holds that the gospel is spoken on the right side of the altar (Bottomley 1978). Here, the use of space, rather than any fixed point within it, is the primary designate of location.

No Direct Correspondence Exists between a Request for Burial and the Grave Site Ultimately Occupied By a Testator

Three kinds of statements suggest that a request for burial in a particular location does not actually indicate the position of the grave site in that space. In cases of "multiple choice" where more than one place of burial may be available to a testator, we are also confronted with the fact that we cannot know where the body of the testator actually comes to rest. We cannot identify a position in space that coincides with a grave or with the body contained therein. We lack the point of reference for location that we seek.

A case in point is that of Alonso Robles. He leaves the choice of grave location to his executors only to add that they might keep in mind that the graves of his father and his father's father are to be found in the

---

[6] Magdalena de Reinoso, 1586, AHPM, Prot. 183, fols. 370r.-371v.
 ...junto a la pila de agua bendita que esta a la puerta de la dicha yglesia... .
[7] Catalina Gomez, 1566, AHPM, Prot. 517, 202r.-203v.
 ...en una sepultura que se abra para este efecto junto a las rejas del altar mayor que ahora esta en la dicha yglesia, o donde estuviere hecho el dicho altar mayor, quando yo fallesciere... .
[8] Francisco de Vera, 1568, AHPM, Prot. 515, fols. 185r.-187r.
 ...en la sepultura que esta en el coro alado del evangelio como entran a donde esta enterrado Maria Ortega mi madre... .

church of Santa Maria. Two others besides are in the church of Santa Maria del Almudena. One belongs to his mother and his maternal grandparents, the one "that is next to the entry door at the stoup of Holy Water in the nave of the Crucifix and the other in the same nave where Ynes de Orozco, my wife who is in heaven, is buried". [9]

Secondly, many requests for burial in a particular location give no specific information other than the name of the building in which the burial is to be located. It may be that the choice of the actual space to be occupied by the grave is left to the testators' executors, or nothing more is said about it. Again, we are unable to produce the site definition that we are conditioned to look for.

In other instances, a location as we understand it in the sense of site definition may appear to correspond with the terms of the request for burial as it is given in the text. "In the chapel, next to the altar" sounds quite promising, until we come across the tell-tale phrase "wherever my executors decide". We cannot locate the grave that marks the spot, for all we have been given here is an indication of a locale.

One Location is not Equivalent to Another Simply Because Each "Fills" a Similar Space

The argument we saw earlier, that space is often characterized on a non-material plane, may be extended to include all statements in which descriptive qualifiers appear in the text. They denote specific locations in that spaces equivalent in kind are thus differentiated from one another. A simple example is provided by Petronilla de Tapia, who asks that she be buried "in the chapel of the baptism".[10] Her grave, like those of many other testators, shall be in a chapel. Unlike others however, her grave is to be found in the chapel of the Baptism.

Seeking the Essence of Location in Testators' Criteria of Representation

All of the above can be re-stated in a more positive way using further examples that I shall discuss below. The very process of doing so signals a radical departure from our old ways of thinking about space and location. We move from an understanding of space that may be summed up by the phrase "site definition", to a less confined view, where space is better understood within the framework of an identity that goes beyond the material constituents of the site itself.

Location May Be Identified as a Grave Plot

We have already considered the example provided by Diego de Buitrago. There are a couple of variations on this type of statement to be added here. Luisa de Velasquez asks to be buried in the place and space wherever a grave is bought,[11] while Juan Garcia simply says that he will be laid in the grave that is given to me."[12] In both instances the expression of location is no more than a reference to the grave itself.

Location May Be Identified as Vicinity

I think of vicinity in those instances where a grave is requested somewhere close (we don't know exactly how close) to another named object. This is as far as we get in understanding location in a statement such as "behind the [burial] niche of señor Martin of this said town, wherever my executors would like".[13]

---

[9] Alonso de Robles, 1605, AHPM, Prot. 1432, fols. 531r.- 533v.
...en la sepultura de la yglesia o monesterio que fuere la voluntad de mis albaceas, no embargante que en la yglesia de Santa Maria desta dicha villa de Madrid tengo sepultura donde estan enterrados mi padre y abuelo de parte de mi padre y en la yglesia de San Gines della tengo dos sepolturas, la una donde estan enterrados mi madre y mis aguelos de parte de mi madre, que es junto a la puerta de la entrada de la pila de agua bendita en la nave del crucifijo y la otra en la mesma nave donde esta enterrada Ynes de Orozco, mi muger que esta en el cielo... .
[10] Petronilla de Tapia, 1559, AHPM, Prot. 311, fols. 254r.-258v.
...en la capilla del bautismo... .
[11] Luisa Velazquez, 1555, AHPM, Prot. 150, fols. 446r.-447v.
...en la parte e lugar donde se compre sepultura... .
[12] Juan Garcia, 1491, AHPS, Prot. 9.19, fols. 20r.
...en la sepultura que me fuere dada... .
[13] Pedro, 1450, AHPS, Prot. 9.1, fols. 3r.-4r.

Here we are given to understand that the grave is located in an approximate relationship with the grave of another, but we do not know the actual distance of the grave from that marker, nor do we know the particular direction in which it lies.

Location May Be Identified as a Spot Located in Relation to Other Criteria

A spot located in relation to other criteria is an expression of location that is more specific than one about vicinity with regard to characterization of space, but not so specific as to yield a definitive understanding of where the grave is. The criteria may include grave patterning in relation to particular material landmarks within the church, or they may refer to economic considerations in the examples that I now present.

Several points in space are represented in Lorenzo Basa de Silva's description of "the grave that is in the first row right up against the Gospel pillar beside the pulpit".[14] These points include the plots laid out in that first row, as well as the Gospel pillar and the pulpit itself. When combined together in a single statement these phrases can be interpreted to mean that the grave is in fact the last one in the first row of graves that extend to the Gospel pillar, the one [the pillar] next to the pulpit. An alternative reading might be that the grave is the last one in the first row. It is up against the Gospel pillar, which also puts it [the grave] next to the pulpit. Either interpretation is possible, given the text that we have, which means the site of the grave itself is still open to question, even though the space around it has been defined by mention of some very specific markers.

An example of a statement in which a grave is located in space in relation to economic criteria is provided by Lope de Mata, who asks that "a grave be bought in the part of the church that costs the least, at the discretion of my executors".[15] Along similar lines we also have the example of Maria Ruiz, who wants a grave purchased "in the best part of the church, no matter what it costs".[16] As above, a space within the church has been described in such a way that it corresponds to a particular area when considered from the point of view of the ground up, but again we do not have enough information to be able to pinpoint the grave site itself.

Location May Be Identified as Somewhere Between Distinctive Features

Expressions of location placed under the above rubric differ from those considered under vicinity and those in relation to other criteria. Location is not gauged by degrees of distance or by placement in a certain spatial context. A statement referring to a destination located somewhere between distinctive features describes the space between two points in which the grave will be placed. Space is more congruent with actual grave location in Juan Marcos request for a plot "that shall be bought in the body of the church and may it be laid in [the space that] is left from the Altar of Our Lady of the Stars until the pulpit".[17] The same may be said of Alonso de Haro's request for a grave "that is close to where the altar is put in the choir, in front and to the right of the crucifix of the said church".[18] In both of these instances the range of possible difference between locating the space described and the grave within it is much more restricted than is the case with earlier examples.

...atras de la nicha del señor Martin desta dicha ciudad a donde mis albaceas quisieren... .
[14] Lorenzo Basa de Silva, 1559, AHPM, Prot. 1420, fols. 504r.-507v.
...en la sepultura que esta en la primera hilera arrimada al pilar del evangelio junto al pulpito... .
[15] Lope de Mata, 1557, AHPM, Prot. 152, fols. 716r.-717v.
...donde se compre una sepultura en la parte que dentro de la dicha yglesia menos costare y ha de ser al parescer de mis albaceas... .
[16] Maria Ruiz, 1581, AHPM, Prot. 1166, unpaginated.
...en la mejor parte de la yglesia, cueste lo que costase... .
[17] Juan Marcos, 1593, AHPM, Prot. 1804, fols. 206r.-209r.
...mando que se compre en el cuerpo de la dicha yglesia y que sea en lo que se dexe desde el altar de Nra. Sra. De Las Estrellas hasta el pulpito... .
[18] Alfonso de Haro, 1458, AHPS, Prot. 9.3, fols. 8v.-11r.
...cerca de donde se pone el altar en el coro frente e derecho al crucifijo de la dicha yglesia... .

Location May Be Identified with Somebody's Grave

A grave identified as that containing the remains of a particular person who may or may not be related to the testator is sometimes used as the primary association for locating a grave within an otherwise unbounded space. In this instance I am not referring to a single grave to be shared between two people, but rather to adjacent graves, in which the space between them is accounted for according to the text. Pedro de Alva describes his grave as "next to that of Francisco Garcia, cleric, the red-haired one".[19] Lazaro Cardiel describes the location of his intended grave in somewhat more detail, by saying that it is "next to the high altar in a plot up from that of his parents' grave, which had been given to him by his aunt".[20]

Location May Be Identified as a Place or Space that is Also Designated by a Particular Association or Name

Here location is expressed in terms of a connection, association or acquaintance that is personal, in the sense of peculiar to the testator rather than necessarily intimate, as we might understand it. Juan Sarga de Cossio asks that his grave be "next to the chapel of the Most Holy Crucifix in [the monastery of] San Felipe, where I keep my ornaments...".[21] The ornaments of which he speaks are the vestments and altar cloths used in his capacity as a priest of the church. To be buried near where these were kept is obviously of some importance to him. It is this emphasis, rather than the fact of burial next to the chapel per se, that really matters with regard to the location of his grave site. The naming of the chapel, however, is not a mere adjunct but a real piece of information, because it is in this chapel and no other that the ornaments are to be found.

Location May Be Identified with a Space that is Designated as a "Traffic Zone"

In this kind of statement location is described in terms of people moving through the grave area. Sometimes motion is expressed by passing through or by a series of named points. Sometimes it is marked by movement from one named space into another. An example of the former is provided by Ynes de Viana, who says that she wants to be buried "in my chapel, which is between the altar and the window, where people go to enter the sacristy".[22] At least four points are named in the foregoing trajectory through space, including the chapel, altar, window and the entrance to the sacristy.

Movement from one named space into another is depicted in Marco de Cores request that he be buried "inside the church in a grave that I have [that is located] as one is leaving the choir on the right hand side".[23] In this instance the named spaces correspond to the body of the church and the choir respectively.

Location May Be Identified as a Space that is Designated by Expression of "Body Pointers"

The criteria of representation expressed as feet, as right hand or left derive from relational concepts. The relations described are not based on approximating the distance from one point to another or the distance between two or more points, or conversely the space that fills a bounded area. They are based on a directional sense that is derived from the mental representation of the body in space and as such they are most straightforward. Juan Salcote wants a grave "at the foot of the church"[24] which could be taken to

[19] Pedro de Alva, 1552, AHPM, Prot. 147, fols. 470r.-472r.
...en la sepultura que alli tengo, junto a la de Francisco Garcia clerigo, el Bermejo... .
[20] Lazaro Cardiel, 1559, AHPM, Prot. 311, fols. 174r.-175v.
...junto al altar de Nuestra Señora en una sepultura que sube de sus padres, que me la dio mi tia... .
[21] Juan Sarga de Cossio, 1602, AHPM, Prot. 1427, fols. 552r.-554r.
...junto a la la capilla del Santo Crucifijo en San Felipe adonde paresciere a mis albaceas, adonde tengo mis ornamentos... .
[22] Ynes de Viana, 1508, AHPM, Prot. 19, unpaginated.
...en mi capilla que esta entre el altar y la ventana por donde entran a la sacristia... .
[23] Marcos de Cores, 1529, AHPM, Prot. 55, fols. 797r.-v.
...dentro de la yglesia en una sepultura que yo tengo en saliendo del coro a mano derecha... .
[24] Juan Salcote, 1531, AHPM, Prot. 111, unpaginated.
...a los pies de la dicha yglesia... .

mean the area at the opposite end of the church from where the altar is located. Juan de Garcia wants a plot" next to the grave of my father on the left hand side".[25] Finally, Juan Cobo wants to be buried "in the cemetery of the church of San Pedro at the door at the foot of the church to the right of where my father was interred".[26] As we see here, there is no limit on how many directional statements may be combined in one description of the same space.

Location May Be Identified as an Area Defined by Association with the Sacred Word

In an area defined by association with the sacred word, location is represented not so much by movement through space but by motion or action in one particular place. The action of preaching the Gospel on the right hand side of the altar and reading from the Epistles on the left (Bottomley 1978) renders the space to the right and left of the altar unique and desirable for burial by association with the sacred. Thus Melchor de la Peña wants to be laid "in the burial plot that the said church has, which is to the side of the High Altar where the Gospel is said".[27] Alonso Lopez wants "the grave that I have pointed out, which is in the hollow of the altar next to the vault on the Epistle side".[28]

In both instances the criteria of representation overlap with the archaeological recognition of material features in that altars are key to both locations. They also overlap with body pointers as outlined above, but these specifics are additions to the operative distinction which is that what is done here draws everything and everyone in the vicinity into a sacred space.

Location May Be Identified as an Area Associated with Religious Practitioners or with a Particular Gender

Areas defined by association with religious practitioners and by association with a particular gender also derive their criteria of representation from the use of space. The primary identification of such a space is premised on the people who use it rather than the action that they take. All of the examples that I cite here involve choirs used by particular sets of people. Alonso de Toledo asks for a grave "in the friars' choir",[29] while Ysabel Ortiz wants one "inside the nuns' choir, at the door where they go out".[30] Finally, Martin Sarmiento wants to be buried "in the men's choir in the grave of my wife".[31] All of these examples suggest once again that while a given location, such as a choir, may have some correlate in a physical setting - meaning that entry and exit through the choir set boundaries on what is choir space and what is not - the real distinction is rooted in a social context which may or may be represented in any material way.

Location May Be Identified with an Object

The point made above may be echoed with regard to those testators who express grave location in terms of proximity to objects that are defined by no more than a name. Bartolome Çerca knows whereof he speaks when he talks of the grave "that I have in front of the Jesus"[32], but we do not. Sometimes the object named is mentioned in relation to another physical feature, as in Maria Lopes' request for a grave

---

[25] Juan de Garcia, 1546, AHPM, Prot. 211, fols. 929r.-932r.
...junto a la sepultura de mi padre a la mano izquierda... .
[26] Juan Cobo, 1554, AHPM, Prot. 149, fols. 375r.-376v.
...en el cementerio de la yglesia de Señor San Pedro deste dicho lugar a la puerta de los pies en derecho de donde se entero mi padre... .
[27] Melchor de la Peña, 1580, AHPM, Prot. 775, fols. 551r.-555v.
...en enterramiento que la dicha yglesia tiene alado del altar mayor donde se dize el evangelio... .
[28] Alonso Lopez, 1611, AHPM, Prot. 2026, fols. 1415r.-1419v.
...en la sepultura que tengo señalada que es en el hueco del altar que es la boveda al lado della epistolar... .
[29] Alonso de Toledo, 1530, AHPM, Prot. 55, fols. 875r.-876v.
...en el coro de los frayles... .
[30] Ysabel Ortiz, 1522, AHPM, Prot. 7, unpaginated.
...dentro del coro de monjas a la puerta donde salen... .
[31] Martin Sarmiento, 1523, AHPM, Prot. 18, fols. 12r.-13v.
...en el coro de los hombres en la sepultura de mi muger... .
[32] Bartolome Çerca, 1529, AHPM, Prot. 2, fols. 616r.-617r.
...en la sepultura que tengo delante del Jesus... .

"at the altar that is at the foot of where Our Lord Saint Peter is".[33] In this instance location is represented by conferring the identity of a particular object to an altar which stands in proximity to the object itself, yet we are never actually informed as to what the exact nature of that object is. "Saint Peter" might be a polychrome wooden statue set back in a niche, or a stone sculpture, or part of a relief or retable. He could be represented in a painting or a stained glass window, but we have no means of knowing which. All we can assume is that people who were there to see him in that church at the time, would of course know the difference.

Losing the Way to Location

The enigma of location is highlighted through all of the examples that have been considered so far, but here we finally touch on the nub of the problem. All criteria of representation, like those of recognition, are rooted in the material world of space and tangible objects. Unlike archaeological criteria of recognition, the testator's criteria of representation also encompass perceptions of relationship, association and actions within, without and in between those spaces and objects that are derived from lived experience of the actual physical and social context that is referred to in each statement made regarding a desired grave location.

At this distance in time and space we do not have any possibility of access to lived experience of any of these spaces or locations, nor can we reconstruct them on the basis of the information given in the wills. No reference to these criteria in a statement of location will be sufficient to allow us to "find" that grave, were we to apply that description of location to a hypothetical setting of a church. I illustrate my point with several relevant examples.

In each of the following statements, we know that a grave location is being described in relation to one or more points in space that have real material correlates in most actual church settings. The points in space are highlighted in bold text. In addition, some points in space are further referenced by criteria of identity that may mark that spot as unique. These are highlighted in italicized text. The statements translate as follows:

"...in the **grave** that I have in the said **church** which is in front of the **pillar** of the **chapel** of *Our Lady of Charity...*".[34]

"...inside the said **church** in the **choir**, in a **grave** of *my father's* next to the **chapel** of *Juan del Prado...*".[35]

"...in the **chapel** where *Don Enladion de Guevara* is buried...".[36]

In the first statement no less than three distinct spaces, the church, chapel and the grave itself are mentioned. The pillar of the chapel is the point of relation between the location of the grave and the chapel itself. In addition, the chapel is placed within the larger context of the church by naming its avocation to Our Lady of Charity. None of this information is useful in pinpointing the grave in the ground. We do not know where the pillar is in relation to the chapel, nor do we know where the chapel is actually sited in the church.

Analysis of the second statement yields an even greater abundance of defined spaces; four in total, two of which, the grave and the chapel are further associated with particular personal identities. Again the

---

[33] Maria Lopes, 1516, AHPM, Prot. 4, unpaginated.
... al altar que esta a pie de donde esta nuestro señor San Pedro... .
[34] Marina Hernandez, 1609, AHPM, Prot. 1438, fols. 752r.-755r.
...en la sepultura que tengo en la dicha yglesia que esta frontero del pilar de la capilla de Nra. Sra. de la Caridad... .
[35] Catalina, 1528, AHPM, Prot. 55, fols. 706r.-707r.
...dentro de la dicha yglesia en el coro, en una sepultura de mi padre junto a la capilla de Juan del Prado... .
[36] Leonor de Zuñiga, 1614, AHPM, Prot. 2015, fols. 1148r.-1150r.
...en la capilla donde esta enterrado Don Enladion de Guevara... .

church, choir and grave are related in space in terms of containment: we know that the church holds the choir which in turn holds the grave. What we do not know is whether or not the chapel is also contained within the confines of the choir, nor is it clear that the testator's father, identified as the owner of the grave, actually lies buried there. Without such indicators, one might well ask what the phrase "next to the chapel" really signifies in terms of locating a specific plot in close proximity to it. If the father has more than one plot as is suggested in the phrase "in a grave of my father's", this also serves as a challenge to any possible translation of the text into an understanding of the terrain that would enable us to reach the grave site as it is described in the text.

Finally, in the last example, we are given one point of reference in space that is the chapel itself. Unlike the chapels alluded to in the previous examples, this one is not identified on the basis of a saintly avocation or a personal claim to the space enclosed within it. The distinction is subtle but important; here the chapel is simply the space where Don Enladion de Guevara is buried. Where his grave is within the chapel is entirely open to question.

Again we have no way to make sense of location as we would expect to see it in an excavation context. In the absence of personal experience of a particular spatial context, neither a detailed description of the relation between two or more points in space, nor a specific identity associated with any one or more of these points in space, serves to anchor location to any particular hole in the ground to the exclusion of any other. In short, location, as we have conceived it in archaeology, disappears under scrutiny.

Retracing Our Steps with a View to What Lies Ahead

The implications of the material that I have presented in this chapter are highlighted in each of the statements made below. I articulate them as points along a line of thought rather than as a finished argument, because all are open to interpretation. At the same time, they express my own understanding of what may be learned about location, given the resources that we have, that is helpful to the growth of our discipline.

First, every testator refers to location in terms that are contingent upon the recognition of space. It is understood that the text of the will is the medium through which we must interpret space.

Secondly, recognition depends on a mental/verbal/written representation of space as much or more than it does on the visual sensing of the actual physical attributes of that space. I believe this to be the crux of the question of what is location.

Thus we are led to the third point; namely that location is a construct. It is sometimes manifested materially. As we have seen in all chapters so far, archaeologists, including me, tend to focus exclusively on the material manifestations.

Finally, the nexus of any statement regarding location is not merely where the grave is, but how to arrive at it in space. People everywhere have understood location in this way, but in archaeology we have lost touch with this nuance, because we do not favor the language of indeterminacy or because "getting to" a space is not self-evident in spatial data.

CHAPTER 5. INDIVIDUAL ACTION: OBSERVING CONTINGENCY IN THE WILLS AND IDENTITY AT THE GRAVE SITE

I argue that a working model of action can be derived from limited evidence by putting ourselves in the shoes of a person who wishes to act. Or, as in the case of the testator, in the shoes of someone who seeks to direct the action of his or her executors in order that his or her will may be carried out sometimes long after death. We must understand all action described in the wills as future, rather than past action. Only then can we get to the crux of the matter, which is to say that no action is independent of space and time. The lynch pin that fixes action to space and time is nothing less than the realization that the testator must preserve an identity in the grave in order that action be undertaken on his or her behalf.

Under this rubric I go on to explore texts that refer to actions, objects and requests for relative placement of the body that somehow serve to mark or distinguish the identity of the testator in the grave. I take a close look at mention of ritual activity and requests for the placement of permanent markers or perishable objects at or on the grave site at specific intervals. My aim is to make a compelling case for the reality of individual action as a prime mover in the formation and interpretation of any archaeological context.

Observing Action in the Text

What we have in the wills is a record of action taken, for a purpose that it was in everyone's interest to fulfill (i.e. to dispose of a corpse). What we know about the execution of these wills is that testators' particular requests for funeral and burial arrangements as set down in the wills were honored as law, and would be carried out to the letter, unless some circumstance prohibited compliance with last wishes. In this regard, no statement made in the text is arbitrary with respect to the testator's intention that an action be carried out on his or her behalf at death or anytime afterwards. In other words, any statement of intended action made by the testator is "the bottom line".

Intended Action

Francisco de la Bandera says unequivocally that he wishes to be buried always in the church of Mojades in his parents' grave. He intends to be buried there if he dies within a ten-league radius of the town. If he should die farther away, he asks to be buried in any church that is dedicated to Saint Catherine, or if not, in one where there is an altar in her name.[1] His intention is quite clearly marked in the text by setting boundaries that are measurable in physical space, for he prefaces this alternative by saying: "...and in some other place outside the ten leagues... from Mojades".[2] Intent in the context of the present example implies more than mere expectation: it suggests a determination to secure a desired outcome despite the vagaries of personal circumstance.

Action and Intent: A Connection Surmised But Not Recorded

Intent may be recognized and distinguished in the text as it is written, but admitting this is not equivalent to knowing what the testator will do or even exactly why he will do it. To say that Francisco de la Bandera may want to be buried in Mojades because of a strong attachment to his parents, or that the alternative suggests that he has considerable devotion to Saint Catherine is to extrapolate intent where none has been recorded.

---

[1] Francisco de la Bandera, 1585, AHPM, Prot. 115, unpaginated.
...que sea sepoltado siempre en el dicho lugar de Mojades a diez leguas alrededor que sea sepoltado en la yglesia de Santa Maria de la dicha villa en las sepolturas de mi padre e madre...e en otra parte fuera de las diez leguas...de Mojades mando que mi cuerpo sea sepoltado en el lugar donde fallesciere en la yglesia que oviere vocacion de Santa Catalina, o al menos altares de su ystoria delante del dicho altar, e den por la sepultura lo que concertaren...
[2] Francisco de la Bandera, loc. cit.

The Existence of Text in Connection with Action and Identity

Nor is it necessary to postulate any special connection here between Francisco de la Bandera as a person, his specific intent and the action, (whichever one it happens to be) that is carried out according to his dictates. We don't need to know anything about who he was in order to know that he did exist, and that things happened because he lived (i.e. he wrote a will) and also because he died (i.e. somebody had to bury him in one of the places that he asked for). It is the fact of individual identity, rather than the postulation of intent in any given text that is essential to incorporating "individual action" into our thinking.

My true starting point for placing the individual at the center of the action in archaeology on the basis of partial evidence lies in the understanding that the text records the will of a person who directs the actions of others in specific ways beyond the frame of his or her earthly existence. Wills are not created to provide us with a record of events and their probable outcomes. All subsequent discussion of contingency, identity and the mediating effects of individual and particular actions on space and time, as explored through various texts unfolds from the preceding insight.

Accounting for Action

The fact that we do not have any statement of specific preference in Francisco de la Bandera's list of alternative grave sites, leads me to consider other texts containing similar ambiguities regarding the ultimate destination of the body from a different angle. Shifting one's sights from a focus on outcomes to a considered emphasis on directed action is the only way to account for all those cases in which a testator suggests more than one alternative as a locale for burial. Contingency - the possibility that something happens depending on some other chance event, encounter or circumstance that has occurred or is likely to take place - is a strong element in all of the examples that we are about to review.

Gaspar de Planiger: The Primacy of Availability

Perhaps Gaspar de Planiger provides the most spectacular example of this type of statement. He describes no less than three options for burial in terms so detailed that his deliberation on the subject of where to put his body to its final rest, cannot be doubted. I quote and paraphrase him at length, as follows: "... when it please God to take me from this present life...if I am in Guadalajara, or some fifteen or twenty leagues away from it in the surrounding countryside, may my body be buried in the church of Santa Ysabel in the chapel left by the secretary Diego Garcia, my lord...". According to his account, the regidor Luis Gernandez is now said to be the patron of the chapel. Gaspar begs the mercy of the latter: "...that he well remember that in life and in death, I have chosen the said grave".

On the other hand, "if God should dispose of my life in the town of Saldaña or somewhere within seven leagues of it", may my body be taken to the church of Santa Maria del Castillo in that town, to be buried in the chapel of Santa Luzia...and if not, in front of the high altar of the same church. If, as Gaspar put it, such "an honest and secure grave cannot be had, then I order that my flesh be laid in the church of San Miguel...next to the marble by the High Altar step", which belongs to the chapel of San Miguel.[3]

---

[3] Gaspar de Planiger, 1530, AHPM, Prot. 55, fols. 841r.-845v.
...quando Dyos fuere servido de me llevar desta presente vida, si adelante en otro testamento o codicilio otra cosa no mandare, que hallandome en Guadalajara o quinze o veinte leguas alrededor, mis carnes sean sepoltadas en la yglesia de senora Santa Ysabel en la capilla que dexo el secretario Diego Garcia mi señor, y mi señora su muger e la doto e ordeno. De la qual dizen que es agora patron el señor regidor Luis Gernandez al qual pido por merced que lo aya por bien presente que en la vida y en la muerte las escogi y que sea del por la dicha sepultura.
...si Dios dispusiere de mi en la villa de Saldaña syete leguas al rededor, que mi cuerpo sea llevado a la yglesia de Santa Maria del Castillo de la dicha villa e alli sea sepultado en la capilla de Santa Luzia si estuviere pa ello y si no delante del altar mayor de la dicha yglesia. En qualquier parte que sea sepultado, sea en el habito de San Francisco y me lo vistan antes que muera, e si no oviere tal enterramiento honesto y seguro pa adelante, mando que mis carnes sean sepultadas en la yglesia del señor San Miguel de la dicha villa, junto al marmol de la grada del altar mayor, que es de la capilla del señor San Miguel... .

The text of Gaspar de Planiger's will is suggestive of directed action based on the possibilities that are available now. "Now" is construed as the means and the people available in a given place to carry out the testator's will regarding burial at the time of his or her death. Contingency surfaces with factors involved in the ultimate location of a grave that remain open-ended until they are acted upon. Death itself, when and where it may occur, is the great unknown, the one event on which all action hinges, in the examples discussed below.

Maria de Avalos: The Primacy of the Executor

For Maria de Avalos, the decision to act depends on the selection of a particular person as executor. She leaves the choice of her grave site to her husband, but if he is not around at the time, she goes on to say that she wants to be buried in the parish to which the house where she should die belongs. She further takes matters into her own hands by stipulating that a grave be bought for her inside the church.[4]

Ana de Herrera: The Primacy of Family Proximity

Sometimes, the course of action to be taken is subject to whether or not the body of a person is present in a given place. Ana de Herrera asks to be buried where her husband is, in the church of Santa Maria de Almudena. If his body does not happen to be there she says she will settle for whatever is "most convenient", or for burial in her father's grave, which is in a chapel of the same church.[5]

Ynes Gomez de Salmeron: The Primacy of a Means of Transport

Sometimes, the resources of the living must also be taken into account. Ynes Gomez de Salmeron directs her executors to bury her with her husband, in Alcalá de Henares, at some distance from Madrid. If they are not equipped to do that, she asks to be buried in the monastery of Nuestra Señora de la Victoria, where her son is. Here again, any prospective action is contingent on conditions that apply at the time of the testators' death.[6]

Melchor de La Peña and Miguela de San Juan: The Primacy of Place of Death

Another prime consideration for action from beyond the grave seems to be place of death. For Melchor de la Peña and Miguela de San Juan respectively, the ultimate choice between burial in Madrid and burial in another town depends on where they happen to be when their moment of truth arrives. Melchor says that if he should die "in the town of Madrid where I have my house, may my body be buried in the monastery of Santa Clara in the grave of my parents-in-law".[7] If the same fate befalls her in Madrid, Miguela asks for burial "in the monastery church of La Santissima Trinidad, in a grave next to the altar of Espiritu Santo".[8]

---

[4] Maria de Avalos, 1554, AHPM, Prot. 150, fols. 419r.-420v.
...en la parte e lugar que a mi marido paresciere e si el no estuviere presente a aqella sazon, me entierren en la yglesia donde fuera parroquiana la casa en que muriere, e se compre una sepultura como sea conveniente dentro de la dicha yglesia... .

[5] Ana de Herrera, 1564, AHPM, Prot.. 314, fols.509r.-510v.
...en Santa Maria del Almudena donde esta enterrado mi marido y si fuere el caso que no estuviere alli me podre enterrar en ella que mas conviene o en la sepoltura donde esta enterrado mi padre en la dicha yglesia que es en la capilla de Nuestra Senora... .

[6] Ynes Gomez de Salmeron, 1577, AHPM, Prot. 1166, unpaginated.
...me entierren con mi marido en la Yglesia Mayor de San Iuste en Alcala de Henares y si no hubiera aparejo para me llevar alla me entierren en la yglesia de Nra Sra de la Vitoria donde mi hijo Juan de Cerceda frayle del dicho monasterio esta enterrado, o a donde paresciere a mis albaceas...

[7] Melchor de la Peña, 1564, AHPM, Prot. 515, fols. 7r.-11r.
...en qualquier parte que yo fallesciere fuera de la villa de Madrid, mi cuerpo sea sepultado en el monasterio de la orden del glorioso San Francisco y si no hubiere monasterio de la dicha horden sea sepultado en la iglesia de la parroquia donde yo muriere en la parte e lugar que a mis testamentarios paresciere e si fallesciere en la villa de Madrid donde yo tengo mi casa, mi cuerpo sea sepultado en el monasterio de Santa Clara en la sepultura de mis senores suegros con el abito de San
Francisco...si muriere en la corte entierren mi cuerpo la cofradia della donde yo soy cofrade y la cruz y clerigos de la parroquia donde fallesciere... .

[8] Miguela de San Juan, 1581, AHPM, Prot. 180, unpaginated.
...si yo fallesciere en Colmenar Viejo sepulten mi cuerpo en la yglesia dela dicha villa donde paresciere a mis albaceas y si fallesciere en Madrid, en la yglesia del monesterio de la Santissima Trinidad, en una sepoltura que esta junto al altar del Espiritu Santo...

If death claims them elsewhere, they have some idea of where they want to secure their final resting-place, though they are not as specific about the details of plot location. The alternatives which they present do not appear to be based on an intimate acquaintance with the ground in which they may lie one day, as was the case with Gaspar de Planiger, but on some notion of the probability of not dying in Madrid.

Melchor de la Peña underscores the impression that this is not a matter of expectation, but an attempt to cover all eventualities. He says "...where ever I die, if it be outside the town of Madrid, let my body be buried in the monastery of the most glorious San Francisco...". He clearly has no idea where he is likely to be if he is not in Madrid, for he goes on to add that if no Franciscan monastery exists in that town, may his body be buried in the church of the parish where he should die.[9] For her part, Miguela simply says: "...if I should die in Colmenar Viejo let my body be buried in the church of the said town wherever my executors decide...".[10] Neither of these people is fixed on any particular outcome. The hour of their death is not imminent, and the setting is as yet unknown, but they are prepared for action in any event.

Menzia Salzedo: The Primacy of Contingency

Action sometimes depends on the expectation that the place where one is living at the time of one's death will not be the place where one has planned to stay for good. I am speaking here of all those testators who request that their bodies be put in temporary deposit prior to transfer and re-interment in a permanent grave at some later date. Such requests are colored by practical considerations imposed by time and distance. Obviously, no executor would be willing, even if he were able, to arrange for the transport of a stinking mass of flesh and many testators may have requested deposit on such grounds.

Menzia Salzedo provides a case in point. She intends to build a monastery, church and chapel for her burial in the city of Granada, far from Madrid, where she is presently drawing up her will. Ever mindful of the uncertainty of events, she discusses the real possibility that her body will have to be placed in deposit "until my bones are clean of flesh".[11] She can count on it, if the chapel is still unfinished at her death, or if the distance proves to be greater than the time elapsed between her death and the first signs of decomposition. To quote her in part "...if it please God that the church is finished before the end of my days, then may my body be taken to the said church and chapel and may it be buried there without being placed in deposit... but if the road... is long, from where I die, and my body cannot be taken there without care and trouble, then let it be deposited...".[12]

The contingency of the present moment and all the variations on this theme free individual action from the realm of abstraction and propel it into a real context of space and time. We are delivered from speculation about anything that is essentially unknowable. We move from asking "where did so-and-so want to end up?" to asking "what are so-and-so's possibilities for action here and now?" I think this brings us much closer to appreciating particular experience as set down in the text. We can better approximate the realities facing the testator, rather than always having to "interpret" and structure our perceptions of this reality. The examples collected above tell us that the testator is directing action according to what may happen in the circumstance of the moment, rather than in expectation of a predetermined outcome.

---

[9] Melchor de la Peña, loc. cit.

[10] Miguela de San Juan, loc. cit.

[11] Menzia Salzedo, 1552, AHPM, Prot. 147, fols. 831r.-839r.
...en un lugar decente en la yglesia o monasterio que a mis testamentarios paresciere como se suele hacer en semejantes casos con las obsequias que a mis testamentarios paresciere que buena y moderadamente se suele hazer por una persona de mediana estado ... yo mando hacer una capilla e yglesia y monesterio para mi enterramiento...y mando que luego que la dicha yglesia y capilla mayor este acabada, mi cuerpo sea llevado y sepoltado en medio de la capilla mayor de la dicha yglesia, y por podria ser que mi fallescimiento fuese pocos dias antes que la dicha yglesia y capilla este acabada y mi cuerpo no estaria para llevar, digo y encargo que lo mas presto que puda ser y mis huesos queden libres de la carne para podellos llevar se lleven...si acahesciere y Dios fuere servido que en mis dias se haga la dicha yglesia, mando que luego que sea fallescida se lleve mi cuerpo a la dicha yglesia y capilla y sea sepultado en el lugar suso dicho sin que sea depositado...si por la distancia del camino donde yo fallesciere hasta la dicha mi yglesia y capilla mi cuerpo no pudiere luego ser llevado sin pesa ni brestonas aya lugar el deposito... .

[12] Menzia Salzedo, loc. cit.

An Argument for Understanding Identity as the Driving Force behind Individual Action in Space and Time

Contingency is still only half the story behind individual action. The other half is identity. There are two sides to this coin. Identity is often perceived as being rooted in a continued, unvarying association in space and time with a particular individual. An example of identity in this sense would be the use of personal names as fixed reference points. Others can recognize us because our association with a name remains consistent throughout life. Our existence, activities, legal status and actual whereabouts can be verified simply by name. This is as true for the dead as it is for the living.

A person is always identified as being the same as we have learned him or her to be. This line of thinking about identity is very comfortable for anyone who seeks to document lives, actions or events that have occurred in the past or in circumstances from which they are geographically removed. Wills and graves are often described as records of one sort or another, and are deemed especially valuable when their connection with a particular person is established by the appearance of that persons' name in other contemporary documents or in an epitaph at the grave site itself. In both instances, the net effect of will or grave seen as "record" puts our understanding of identity as it relates to the individual into a static frame. The individual is "flash-frozen" by the use of a name; he or she becomes a point of placement in space and time.

On the other hand, identity may also be thought of as the on-going creation of self, as we respond to people and situations around us (space) and also to our own internal states, which shift continually and manifest outwardly as we move through the life cycle (time). This continuous tension between constancy and change in identity may be likened to an understanding of what happens to a tree as it lives through the four seasons. In spring a tree opens tender new leaves. As summer approaches it bursts into bloom. By early autumn fruit hangs heavy off those same branches. With the arrival of winter bare boughs are traced against a lowering sky. At each instance the tree appears to be a different being, yet we learn from experience that it is the same entity. It is easy to associate this dynamic aspect of identity with the activities, concerns and aspirations of the living, but it may be less obvious that it also applies to the dead.

In keeping with this dynamic view of identity we may approach the text as an expression of a person's free will. Like any impulse of the living that prompts some action, the will of the dead, as observed by executors, has real consequences in space and time.

Probable though not necessarily inclusive outcomes of the will may include; the selection, creation, and marking of a grave site as well as the burial of bodies in the ground. All of these actions have a detectable impact on any physical setting. Other outcomes of the will that are tied into the creation of an awareness of time include how long and how continuously the grave is distinguished from other graves around it by the use of markers and/or the performance of ritual at the grave site. All such action highlights the realization that time is a relative concept. It passes or seems to stand still, depending on what has been done or left undone. Here I suggest that space and time are mediated by individual action because all action derives from an individual's understanding of his or her identity in the world. Death does not preclude the possibility of effective action in the sense that I have just described.

Resolving Identity: A New Direction of Thought

Before continuing, it is useful to indicate the direction in which we are going. The present chapter consists of an exploration of the following sequence of ideas, drawing on a small selection of the wills at hand. We continue to establish the nature of the connection between an individual's action and his or her identity. The testator may be seen as self-creator of his or her own posthumous identity. The testator may also be depicted as prime mover of any action performed at his or her behest.

We return in both instances to the suggestion made above, that individual action (which stems from identity) is taken to mediate space and time. In so doing, a testator's posthumous identity, his or her particular presence in the awareness of the living as manifested in action addressed to him or her may be resolved in several ways. Identity may dissolve with the passage of time as action taken to distinguish a grave from those surrounding it slowly ceases. On the other hand, identity may be resolved by encroaching on space and time indefinitely. It may be sustained by periodic renewal in actions of remembrance. It may be reinforced by placement of the grave so that the body is absented from or lies in the presence of associations that are given some relative value by the testator. In other instances, identity seems never to be lost or diminished by death, as the testator assumes the continued integration of his or her body and soul, despite the acknowledgment of mortality inherent in leaving a will.

The Testator as Self-Creator

At this juncture the manifestation of identity in space becomes inextricably entwined with the question of locating a particular grave time and time again. Criteria of recognition, those elements of location that are somewhat fixed over a period of time, and criteria of representation, those elements of location that vary depending on ones' perception of the space described, as discussed in the preceding chapter, come into play here. The testator may evoke use of these criteria to establish a presence that encourages an active response from the living in varying degrees and combinations, depending upon the resources he or she is able and willing to command. The wills of Maria Hurtado and Diego Daça provide us with enough detail to present our case.

Maria Hurtado: Maintaining the Status Quo in Death as in Life

For Maria Hurtado, a posthumous identity appears to consist of a continuing association with her husband in death. She is to be buried in the chapel founded by him. Her body will be laid in the plot next to his. She wants a flat stone level with the floor, whereas her husband's grave is to be marked with a sculpture or statue. No mention is made of any other graves there. She also asks that a stone plaque be affixed to the wall of their chapel. The purpose of this plaque is, as she puts it, to ensure that her descendants always pay to keep the lamp of the most Holy Sacrament lit, thus "a-lighting her soul and that of her husband". It is also inscribed with a reminder that the feast of Our Lady of the Conception is to be observed in the chapel every year in perpetuity.[13]

Diego Daça: Disdaining the Flesh to Honor the Soul

Diego Daça's posthumous identity appears to be based on the shedding of worldly attachments to the flesh. His grave is laid in the most traveled public space imaginable, within the doorway of the church. His is a most deliberate decision, for he insists: "Let my body be buried in this grave and in no other".[14]

---

[13] Maria Hurtado, 1515, AHPM, Prot. 4, unpaginated.
...mando que junto a la sepultura del dotor mi senor que santa gloria aya sea sepultado mi cuerpo como dicho tengo e que no pongan sobre mi sepoltura una losa mia sino una piedra llana junto con el suelo....
Mando que sobre el sepulcro del dotor pongan un bulto de piedra labrada... mando que myll mrs que yo tengo de censo sobre las casas de Garcia de la Pena den en cada un ano para siempre novecientos mrs para azeite a la lampara del Santissimo Sacramento que en la dicha yglesia esta por quien plega a el de alumbrar mi anima e la del doctor e los otros difuntos de donde yo desciendo. E los otros cien maravedies que quedan de los dichos myll mrs mando que se den en cada un ano a pitanca a los clerigos que serieren la dicha yglesia por que en mi nombre ede los otros mis difuntos celebren en cada un ano para siempre, una fiesta de la Santissima Concebicion de Nra. Sra., la qual fiesta haran despues del dia de su fiesta, tres dias o quatro....mando por qual dicha lampara se provea e aya siempre memoria e la dicha fiesta se celebre que se ponga en una piedra escrita esta cosa, mando que de los dichos myll maravedies, e sea puesta e metida en la pared de la Capilla de nuestro enterramiento en manera que le puede bien leer por que mis descedientes leyendolo, sepan que en mano de cada uno de ellos esta en hazer que se provea e repare la dicha lampara, e se gasten los dichos 900 mrs en hazeite para que sea proveydo, e se celebre la dicha fiesta de la Concebicion por los dichos cien maravevedis que restan de los dicho myll maravedies...mando que se faga un caliz de plata e una patena, que pese todo dos marcos e medio de plata e que el calice sea dorado por de dentro e los bevedos e que lo den para con que se celebre el Santissimo Sacramento en la capilla del dicho Dotor e mio e en la dicha yglesia para siempre jamas, e quemado mas un par de candeleros de Azofre, lo qual todo es lo que el dicho doctor e mi senor e yo ovimos mandado en el dicho testamento...que el dicho caliz e candeleros e todos los otros hornamentos que yo aya dado e mandare dar este empoder e a cargo del cura, que es o fuere como los otros hornamentos de la dicha yglesia para que con ellos se celebre el oficio divino en la dicha nuestra capilla e la dicha yglesia se sirva dellos quando los oviere menester e la capilla del senor Martin Diego Goncales que Santa Gloria aya... .
[14] Diego Daça, 1607, AHPM, Prot. 1435, fols. 15r.-16r.
...en la yglesia del dicho monasterio, junto a la puerta de la yglesia y en el medio de ella. En esta sepoltura sea mi cuerpo sepoltada y no en otra ninguna y en la dicha sepoltura se ponga una piedra que es mia, y esta puesta en el claustro del dicho monesterio, junto a la puerta que sale

To continue with the words of a fellow testator named Pedro de Castillo, this may be so that "all who enter in [the church] step on the earth where my body shall be".[15]

The logic behind the situation of the grave in such a spot may derive from the very old idea that burial outside the west door of the church "could be a deliberate act of humility" (Colvin 1991:127). It may also have something to do with the exaltation of the soul at the expense of denigrating the body. Something of these sentiments is expressed in the published account of the last will and testament of Miguel de Mañara, founder of the Hospital de la Caridad in Seville, who died in 1679. He asks to be laid outside the church door where all must walk over him, for as he puts it, "...may my filthy body, unworthy to be inside the temple of God, be buried there".

Along the lines of letting go of all material corruption, while safeguarding the fate of the soul, Daça's grave stone carries an image of death and the Latin words, "orate pro eo" already carved into it. He also asks that only the day, month and year of his death be added to this exhortation and nothing more, not even his own name, "...no sign, nothing other than the clean surface of the stone itself, with these things declared upon it".[16] Identity is subverted here in the guise of anonymity.

In his request for anonymity, coupled with the reminder to pray for his soul, Diego Daça prefigures Miguel de Mañara's epitaph to some extent, though Mañara's refusal to name himself is again an expression of contempt for all the things of this world. According to Mañara's will, his gravestone must read: "Here lie the bones and ashes of the worst man there has ever been in the world. Pray to God for him".

On a final note, the commemoration of Daça's soul is a brief, but intensive affair. In contrast to Maria Hurtado, he asks that all masses for his soul, including that which is sung on the first anniversary of a person's death, be compressed into the three days immediately following his burial, with no further ado.[17]

One Last Look at Maria and Diego: Collapsing Space and Time in Identity

The identification and manner of placement of their graves as well as the intervals of ritual attention requested suggest that Maria Hurtado and Diego Daça have devised two very different strategies for acting on space and time. In the case of the former, action is parlayed into the enclosed space of the chapel, where Maria and her husband are forever unchanging, contained in memory through the lamp that is always lit, the inscription on the wall, and the feasts kept in perpetuity. Space and time collapse in a time-capsule effect.

Diego Daça's grave is situated in the midst of the high road of the church. It is positioned so that the potential for receiving the blessings and prayers of all churchgoers at any and all times is virtually unlimited. Action is directed to the ceaseless remembrance of his soul, which is to say the eternal self, obviating the need for identifying its' temporary mortal shell. Space and time collapse in a round of continuous motion.

---

del dicho claustro a la capilla mayor. Mandando quitar y borrar della las letras que estan escriptas en la cabeca de la dicha piedra y al fin della, dejando tan solamente en la dicha piedra la muerte que esta esculpida en ella, con las letras que dizen <orate pro eo> y el dia, mes y ano de mi fallescimiento, y no otra cosa, ni nombre, ni senal sino la piedra linpia, con estas cosas aqui declaradas... .

[15] Pedro de Castillo, 1606, AHPM, Prot. 2015, fols. 1170r.-1214v.

... si Dios fuere servido de llevarme de este presente vida en esta ciudad de San Christoval de la Havana mi cuerpo sea sepoltado en el monasterio del senor San Francisco en medio de la puerta principal de la yglesia del monasterio y umbrales della para que todos los que en ella entraren pisen la tierra donde estuviere mi cuerpo, y lo mesmo sea en qualquier parte e lugar de los Reinos de Espana e destas Yndias donde fallesciere, que mi entierro a de ser en el monasterio de Senor San Francisco, en la parte e puerta principal de la yglesia donde muriere... .

[16] Diego Daça, loc. cit.

[17] Diego Daça, 1605, AHPM, Prot. 1432, fols. 577r.-580v.

...en los tres dias que se digan las misas se cubre mi sepoltura con un pano negro que diga vacanttes Renglones dies vala...puesto sobre la tumba que a de estar puesta en la sepoltura, y en ella se ponga quatro hachas de cera que esten encendidas mientras las misas se dijeren y quattro velas de cera de a media libra y acabada la misa se salga con el responso sobre mi sepultura y despues de acabado el novenario de las dias nueve misas rezadas de nra. sra., se haga el cabo de año por mi anima... .

It may be said for both Maria Hurtado and Diego Daça that the construct of identity itself is largely derived from the placement of the grave in space in such a way that it serves the living to act in remembrance of them. With every instance of acknowledgment they receive from priests, from their posterity, or from passers by, they succeed in collapsing space and time. The repeated renewal of their identity in the present, that is to say in the moment that something is done on their behalf, defeats the constraints of mortality.

CHAPTER 6. THE INTERPLAY AMONG ACTION, IDENTITY, SPACE, TIME AND MATERIAL REMAINS: THE TESTATOR AS PRIME MOVER OF THE ACTION

By way of reinforcing what has not been made explicit in the examples given so far, I note here that the testator, the very person whose remains we uncover in the grave, is the "prime mover" of all action pertaining to the disposition of his or her body and the care of his or her soul, regardless of who actually does the walking and talking and also regardless of whether any such action is mentioned in the text at all or made visible in the ground. In the examples just discussed and in what is left to come, we can see that material, temporal and spatial elements are variously drawn together in the making of a posthumous identity construct that is contingent on particular actions carried out in specific locations at certain times by others on the testator's behalf.

A testator may make use of material elements, objects that are placed in particular patterns of association in space, so as to create, continue or re-create an identity. Such an identity may encompass remembrance of the testator as a person as with Maria Hurtado, or simply as one among the dead in the minds of others as in the case of Diego Daça. Such objects may be perishables or not, impermanent or not, moveable or transferable or not. They may include the use of food, drink, light, dress, ornament, monuments, images, paintings and epitaphs, etc. to preserve, capture or highlight the present moment for the moment or in eternity as will be seen below.

A testator may also make use of ritual actions that take place within specific intervals of time that may or may not be associated with the space occupied by his or her grave. He or she may use ritual actions to create, continue or re-create an identity, or a remembrance of the testator as a person, or simply as one among the dead in the minds of others. The testator may make use of intervals that are set by convention, or he or she may request an abbreviation, or a prolonged repetition of such ritual action. Masses, sung or chanted, responses said, prayers made on behalf of the deceased, devotions observed on a daily, weekly, monthly or yearly basis, in perpetuity or for a limited time only, at the grave or at an altar, chapel or at some place of pilgrimage; all may serve to anchor identity in time and space. Again we leave specific examples for a later point in the chapter.

A testator may make use of the placement of his or her own body in space, so as to create, continue or re-create an identity, or a remembrance of the testator as a person, or simply as one among the dead in the minds of others. The terms of definition of this body space in association with the testator's cast of mind regarding the link between body, soul and self are a matter of guesswork at best. We will consider quite a few examples in which a certain tension between intimations of mortality and hopes of eternity appear to be focused on a concern for where the body is laid in relation to other bodies, other dead, or others still living, rather than on or in addition to objects or actions that are brought into association with it.

The Interplay among Action, Identity, Space and Time: The Passage of Time as Expressed in Offerings

Identity comprises relationships set up between any two or more of the following: action, objects, body, soul, grave (space), self and time. In the examples which follow, action may be directed in such a way that the testator's individual identity is ultimately dissolved in space and time. The dominant image here is passage: we may think of the leaf as it falls from the tree. For Elvira Rodriguez, Luis Monte de Colmenar, Pedro Tomano, Balthasar Gaviña, Francisca de Xalon and Mari Lopez, identity is linked to action insofar as the ultimate release of soul, or letting go of the need to maintain a separate identity within the grave, corresponds with the cessation of action once a particular interval of time has elapsed.

Elvira Rodriguez, Luis Monte de Colmenar and Maria de Pontes: A Year-Long Feast for the Dead

All three ask that bread, wine and candle wax be placed at their grave sites until the first anniversary of their deaths. The actual performance of ritual and the leaving of offerings coincide in space and time at the grave of the deceased. Elvira Rodriguez is most succinct about it, declaring "may they say a response with bread and wine over my grave every Sunday for one year".[1]

Masses appear to be observed at intervals of different lengths and offerings may take slightly different forms. For Luis Monte de Colmenar, like Elvira Rodriguez, the marking of the grave with offerings and responses is to occur once a week.[2] Maria de Pontes asks for the same attentions on a daily basis, "...for a whole year may they say a response and give the priest [un morabe], and burn a whole tablet or candle on the altar and give food to the sacristan...".[3]

Pedro Tomano and Baltasar Gaviña: Slowing the Pace of Consumption over Time

Sometimes the length of an interval between one set of offerings and the next, changes over time. Pedro Tomano asks that bread, wine and candle wax be placed on his grave every day for the first nine days after his death, perhaps in accompaniment to a novenario. After that, his wife is to leave them there every Sunday until the first anniversary of his demise.[4] It is clear that the grave is "marked" not by the placement of perishable goods so much as by the ritual activity that occasions their presence. The same principle governs the use of non-perishable items at gravesites, excepting permanent features like headstones, as we will see later.

Baltasar Gaviña provides another example of the slowing rate of ritual attentions to the grave as the months and years go by. He asks that all the usual ceremonies be carried out at his grave, beginning oblate and candle after the ninth day for a period of two years, according to custom. It is only during the first year that a mass is to be said for him with a response at his grave every day, although anniversary masses are to be said at the end of the first and second years.[5] A corresponding reduction in the "consumption" of bread, wine and wax would create the impression, both for us and for the still-living contemporaries of the dead, that as time flows onward, the deceased are less and less present.

---

[1] Elvira Rodriguez, 1539, AHPM, Prot. 134, unpaginated.
... cada domingo por un año digan un responso sobre mi sepultura... .
[2] Luis Monte de Colmenar, 1542, AHPM, Prot. 210, 234r.-235v.
....cada domingo despues de mi fallescimiento hasta cumplir el primer aniversario de mi muerte, que me lleben sobre mi sepultura en el monesterio pan e vino e cera, mi muger Petonyla Hernadez, o su madre Ursula de Yola, como sea costumbre en Olmedo... .
[3] Maria de Pontes, 1550, AHPM, Prot. 214, fols. 291r.-292.r.
...todo un año cumplido digan un responso, y den al cura un morabe y arde en el altar una tabla o candela de cera todo y den de comer al clerigo y al sacristan... .
[4] Pedro Tomano, 1542, AHPM, Prot. 210, fols. 222r.-223v.
...que nueve dias despues de mi entierro, cada dia dia me lleven pan y vino sobre mi sepultura lo que a mis albaceas les parecen... todos los domingos despues que yo muriere un año entero, mi muger me lleve sobre mi pan e vino e cera, lo que a ella le paresciere....
[5] Baltasar Gaviña, 1594, AHPM, Prot. 1805, fols. 644r.-646r.
... se me hagan en el: el nocturno, novenario, y demas officios acostumbrados, y que acompañen mis honras los señores del cabildo... y pasado el noveno dia, se me comience luego oblada y candela segun costumbre por tiempo de dos años, haciendo cabo de año y de dos anos, y en el primer año se me diga una misa cada dia y aquella dicha el sacerdote diga responso sobre mi sepultura... .

Francisca de Xalon and Mari Lopez: A Brief Passage Marked by Candlelight

This passing, beyond that of physical death, is acknowledged, tacitly or otherwise, in the cessation of ritual attention at the grave site. The grave itself "disappears" in space and time, as it is no longer singled out by acts or offerings from all the other graves around it. Sometimes the oblivion appears to set in immediately following the funeral. The grave is marked with cloth and candles on the day of burial itself, but no further mention is made of commemorating the dead in the place where their body lies after final interment. This is not to say that no masses for the soul were ever sung afterwards but if they were they may not have entailed offerings at the grave site in all instances. Francisca de Xalon refers only to the day of her burial when she asks that lights be placed all around her body, by her grave and on all surrounding altars.[6] On the day that she is buried, Mari Lopez wants two large candles to be placed on her grave, so that they burn in parallel to the cross.[7] In effect, they cease to be once the candles have burned out.

The Interplay among Action, Identity, Space and Time: The Remembrance of Space as Expressed in Reinforcement, Repetition and Renewal of Action

In the examples that follow, action may be directed in such a way that the testator's individual identity ultimately dissolves space and time through repeated remembrances. The dominant image here is renewal; we may think of the leaf on the branch of the tree as it begins life anew every spring. The release of the soul is achieved through the remembrance of space at, around, or in some way associated with the testator's grave. This remembrance of space occurs at particular intervals of time, and is fixed through the repetition of certain actions at those times.

We have just seen how offerings, perishable objects themselves, may mark the passing of the living from space and time in some instances. In other instances, objects may serve to "fix" the memory of the dead in space and time. What is worth noting in this collection of examples is that the memory of the dead may be fixed in space and time with or without the use of gravestones to mark the spot where the body is actually laid. In all of these cases the memory of the dead is "fixed" by the repetition of ritual activity at, or in the vicinity, of the grave at daily, weekly or yearly intervals. No temporal limit is set on this activity; in other words it is expected to be perpetual.

Esteban de Torres and Geronimo de Cuenca: Remembrance of Repeated Actions in Space Written in Stone

There are several ways to "remember" space. For Esteban de Torres and Geronimo de Cuenca, remembrance of space is achieved by performing actions that are repeated without variation at regular intervals over an indefinite period of time. Both request stones not to mark their graves but to commemorate their founding of a chaplaincy and the building of a chapel that will house their bodies and most important, tend to the fate of their souls. The form, placement and general content of these commemorative plaques look to be identical according to the descriptions given in the texts, only that Esteban de Torres is a man of fewer words.[8] Geronimo de Cuenca elaborates a little more:"...may a large white and well-worked stone be set in the place designed for it, underneath the window". He adds, "may the founding of the chapel and chaplaincy and patronage and the names of the founders of all this be written upon it in black letters".[9]

---

[6] Francisca de Xalon, 1627, AHPM, Prot. 4025, fols. 191r.-195r.
... en mi tumba y alrededor della pongan lutos y en todos los altares alrededor della se pongan luces y sobre mi cuerpo y alrededor de la tumba . .
[7] Mari Lopez, 1548, AHPM, Prot. 212, fols. 516r.-516v.
...el dia de mi enterramiento pongan sobre mi sepultura dos hachas de cera que arden a par de la cruz... .
[8] Esteban de Torres, 1606, AHPM, Prot. 1435, fols. 252r.-258r.
...se ponga una piedra blanca grande bien labrada debajo de la ventana y en letras negras dotacion, capellania, patronazgo y nombres de los fundadores de la capilla... .
[9] Geronimo de Cuenca, 1604, AHPM, Prot. 1435, fols. 418r.-425v.
... y se ponga una piedra blanca grande, y bien labrada en el lugar que esta senalado para ella debajo de la bentana, en la qual se escriba con letras negras la dotacion de la dicha capilla, y capellania, y patronazgo, y los nombres de los fundadores de todo ello... .

Ana de Carvajal And Geronima de Montalban: Remembrance of Space Lies in Repeated Actions

In the examples provided by Ana de Carvajal and Geronima de Montalban, space is remembered simply by the repetition of action at their respective graves. Both establish perpetual chaplaincies that are to be performed at their graves, but they do not mention any marker or structure that would distinguish the site from its surroundings. In both cases, the details of which masses are to be said and how often differ, but the "where" remains essentially if not substantially the same. Ana simply says: "...I order that a chapel of one mass be said every day in perpetuity in the monastery of Los Angeles...in the place where my parents are buried and I will be buried as well".[10] Geronima asks that masses be said in perpetuity "...in San Xines... where my parents, ancestors and I, too, am buried...".[11]

Alonso Ruiz Sanchez and Françisca de Alcaniça: Remembrance of Space Renewed with Repeated Actions and Objects Re-Placed at the Grave at Regular Intervals

In the examples provided by Alonso Ruiz Sanchez and Françisca de Alcaniça, space is remembered by repetition of action at fixed intervals, in conjunction with the temporary placement of moveable markers at their respective graves. They ask that their graves be marked on days when masses are said for their souls. Alonso Ruiz is building both a tomb and a chapel to house his remains, so his grave will not easily disappear into the fabric of the church. All the same, he wills that a cloth be bought specially to cover the monument at his grave. It is to remain there for the whole year following his death. After that, it is to be kept in the sacristy and used to drape the tomb only on the days in which the nuns are to say mass for his soul. He notes that their obligations to his memory are detailed in the bill of sale that he has drawn up with them.[12]

Francisca de Alcaniça has a silver cross that she keeps in her oratorio. She wills it to the church or monastery where she is to be buried so that it may serve in that church. She asks only that it be placed atop her grave on the days when a mass is held.[13] Here, a personal possession ceases to be personal, except when the association is revived by several actions. One action is to restore the cross to its original owner by placing it on her grave. Another is to remember her soul in the mass given at the time. And the third is to remove the cross once it is over. In so doing, Francisca de Alcaniça is rendered alive and present, if only for a few brief moments.

The temporal restriction on the use of the cloth and cross in the preceding examples suggests that the function of these objects is not to mark the grave, but to highlight the continued remembrance of the dead in the sacred interval of the mass. The use of objects to mark the grave-space is not incidental in such a context. Whether such items are used by all testators who request masses in perpetuity is a question that I do not know the answer to, but in all the cases considered above, ritual activity at the grave is the primary matter of record. This would suggest to me that personal identity becomes increasingly dependent on the acts of remembrance that it engenders once the cycle of repetition has begun. It is not necessarily invested in material associations, though these are certainly present. Again, we see that the matrix of identity is found in individual action operating in and on space and time.

---

[10] Ana de Carvajal, 1608, AHPM, Prot. 2015, fols. 2036r.- v.
...mando una capilla perpetua de una misa de una misa cada dia en el monesterio de
Los Angeles ...donde mis padres estan enterrados y yo me mando enterrar... .
[11] Geronima de Montalban, 1610, AHPM, Prot. 1430, fols.2379r.-2385v.
... en San Xines... adonde mis padres y difuntos estan enterrados e yo me mando enterrar... .
[12] Alonso Ruiz Sanchez, 1612, AHPM, Prot. 2010, fols. 100r.-103r.
...mando se aga una tumba para que este en mi sepultura y capilla, y se compre para cubrirla un pano de veynte dosino de a tres ducados vara y cite un ano a la continua alli y despues se quite y guarde el pano en la sacristia para que se ponga los dias que las monjas an de hazer las memorias por mi conforme a lo contenido en la venta y escriptura que entre ellas y mi se hizo... .
[13] Francisca Henriquez de Alcaniça, 1598, AHPM, Prot. 1810, fols. 100r-103r
... mando a la yglesia o monesterio donde mi cuerpo estuviere, una cruz de plata que yo tengo en mi oratorio para que sirva en la dicha yglesia, y se ponga encima de mi sepultura los dias de una misa... .

The Interplay between Action, Identity, Space and Time: Eternity of Soul as Expressed in Absence of the Body from a Given Set of Associations

In the examples that follow, action may be directed in such a way that the testator's individual identity ultimately dissolves space and time via the possibility that some remainder of the soul is left within the body for eternity. The presence or absence of the body itself from a certain place appears to be an integral part of one's identity. In the texts that I discuss below, a case might be made for the perception that the placement of the body in a certain space somehow serves as an anchor for the continuity of the identity of that person throughout time. Here I am not just referring to the "social aspect" of burial location, implicit in the desire to be buried in or near the graves of relatives. I focus my attention on all those instances where the testator directs others to act or not to act in such a way that the body, not the grave, is singled out as the locus of identity after death.

Such an identity is established by an act which involves "separation" from some person or category of persons who may or may not be named as significant others according to the testator himself. By asking to be buried in a new grave, or in a grave that is physically removed or of restricted access to others, the testator is thus distancing or separating his or her body from the anonymity of placement among the common mass of burials that would otherwise surround it. Identity premised on separation is never presented as such in any of the texts that I discuss below, but an emphasis on establishing body boundaries in space that in some instances are to be maintained over time may be inferred from each kind of statement that I have just listed. The dominant image here is that of perpetuity; we may think of the body or the trunk of the tree itself, as being rooted in the earth and clinging to the soil through many years.

Juan Perez, Mari Frutos, Bartolome Alfaro, Antonio Nuñez, Antonia and Alfonso Muñoz: Solitude Preferred

In each of the examples that I now present, it is clear that the testator has opted for burial in a grave which for the time being is not occupied by any other body, be it of a spouse, a parent, child or colleague. Juan Perez asks that a plot be purchased inside the church, and "if it could be of earth in which no other body has been buried".[14] The condition of the grave matters more to Juan Perez than its exact whereabouts within the church, for he leaves that decision to his executors.

Mari Frutos has her heart set on a virgin grave in the first row from the doorway inside the church. Here again is the insistence on having an previously unused or "virgin" grave. It appears to be a primary factor in seeking a plot in that locale rather than the locale itself. If such a grave does not exist or cannot be had in that first row, then Mari Frutos is content to let her husband choose her final resting place.[15] Perhaps she has made her selection in the belief that such a grave is more likely to be available in that area. In the absence of any statement about retaining a grave near the doorway, regardless of its past use, this is a fair assumption.

Bartolome Alfaro goes one farther, in asking for a grave that he knows to be unused. He asks for a virgin plot inside the church, but he is more specific about where one actually is than either Juan Perez or Mari Frutos. He names the man who currently occupies the grave next to the one that he intends for himself as Juan de Hinosa.[16] Again, judging by these words, we cannot doubt that burial in such a grave matters more to him than interment in a more exalted place that also happens to be full of bodies. If it were otherwise he would not be that specific.

---

[14] Juan Perez, 1539, AHPM, Prot. 134, unpaginated.
...para enterrar mi cuerpo se compre dentro de la dicha yglesia del monasterio una sepultura e si se pudiere que sea de tierra en que ningund cuerpo se aya sepultado, la qual se pague de mis bienes... .
[15] 15. Mari Frutos, 1542, AHPM, Prot. 212, fols. 516r.- v.
...en la yglesia de San Andres, vocacion del lugar de Villa, en una sepultura virgen en la primera orden de la puerta de los pies y si no oviere virgen, a donde mi marido quisiere....
[16] 16. Bartolome Alfaro, 1551, AHPM, Prot. 214, fols. 277r.-278r.

Antonia and Antonio Nuñez do not ask to be buried in new graves, but they do seek graves that lie in relatively un-crowded ground. Antonia wants to be buried in the rear choir, which is at the foot of the church, "in a place where my grave is made without prejudice to any other grave in the said church".[17] For his part, Antonio Nuñez simply says "wherever space is least filled up".[18] In a slightly different vein, Alfonso Muñoz asks for "the grave, if there is one that is empty of bodies".[19] Whether any of the testators mentioned in the foregoing examples hope that their bodies remain intact by being buried alone, or that no other person be allowed to share their grave in future, is unknowable.

Esteban de Torres and Gaspar Salçedo: By Invitation Only
In other cases, the distinctions become rather more apparent. Separation from the bodies of most if not all others in death is accomplished by setting limits on who else may be buried in one's grave. Esteban de Torres and his wife wish to endow a chapel in the monastery of La Concepcion Geronima, but no matter where they end up, only he and his wife, their siblings and the patrones along with their respective siblings will be allowed interment in the chapel vault.[20] Along the same lines, Gaspar Salçedo asks that he and his wife be interred next to the steps of the High Altar, in a grave reserved "for us alone, forever and ever".[21]

Juana de Luçenberger and Magdalena Ulloa de Sarmiento: Renouncing Family Ties for a Place among the Nuns

With the last part of the preceding quote, a temporal dimension is made explicit. For some testators a separation from all other family members in death is reinforced by this kind of admonition. Juana de Luçenberger, Magdalena Ulloa de Sarmiento and Pedro Zapata de Cardenas insist on remaining in the place where they are to be buried forever and for always, but the circumstances of their wills differ. In Juana's case, she is renouncing the world in order to enter the convent; thus she "gives her body to religion" and in particular to Nuestra Señora de la Concepcion de San Francisco, "where it must always remain".[22] The text in this case connotes a "burial of the living" and by extension, a letting go of all worldly ties and possessions, including remembrance of the body itself, even though Juana de Luçenberger's actual physical death may still be a distant possibility.

Magdalena Ulloa de Sarmiento does not appear to have taken the veil, but she most definitely has secured a grave in the "long" choir of the convent occupied by the discalced nuns of the order of San Geronimo. She begs the foundress of the convent, the Condesa de Castellar, to put her grave in a place where it might be permanent, for "it is her will to remain in the said convent and choir perpetually and also forever within the church of the said convent". Magdalena is so confident that the Condesa will do so that she has "left her parents' grave for this one".[23]

...dentro en la yglesia en sepultura virgen y sea la que esta junto con la sepultura de Juan de Hinosa... .
[17] Antonia, 1551, AHPM, Prot. 214, fols. 328r.-329r.
...en el coro postrero que es a los pies de la dicha yglesia, en parte se haga mi sepultura que esta sin perjuizio de otra sepultura en la qual dicha yglesia... .
[18] Antonio Nuñez, 1554, AHPM, Prot. 215, fols. 161r.-162r.
...donde mas desocupado oviere... .
[19] Alfonso Muñoz, 1466, AHPS, Prot. 9.6, fols. 4r.- 5r.
...en la sepultura si la hay sin enterrados... .
[20] Esteban de Torres, 1604, AHPM, Prot. 1430, fols. 418r.-425v.
...Y queremos que tan solamente en la boveda de la dicha capilla se entierren nuestros
cuerpos, y los de nuestros hermanos y los de los Patrones, y sus mugeres y los de los hermanos del Patron y sus hijos y no mas... .
[21] Gaspar Salçedo, 1583, AHPM, Prot. 180, unpaginated.
...nos entierren junto a las gradas del altar mayor que sea para nosotros solos para siempre jamas... .
[22] Juana de Luçenberger, 1612, AHPM, Prot. 2010, fols. 1042r.-1046v.
....el cuerpo doy a la dicha religion de la Concepcion de Nra Sra de la orden de San Francisco donde ha de permanecer siempre... que es donde ha de permanecer siempre... .
[23] Magdalena Ulloa de Sarmiento, 1618, AHPM, Prot. 2024, fols. 1042r.-1046v.
...en el convento de monxas descalzas de la orden de San Geronimo de mi señora la Condesa del Castellar desta villa de Madrid que es adjunto a la parroquia de San Iuste señaladamente en el coro largo del dicho convento que señalo por entero, y suplico a la dicha mi señora condesa del Castellar hordene donde se ponga y este con decoro y permanencia, como estoy cierta lo hara por la particular me de que en ellome hace que tanto estimo pues dexo el entierro de mis padres por ello...mi voluntad es de quedar en el dicho convento y coro perpetuamente y para siempre y ansi en la yglesia del mismo convento y por las religiosas que ordenare en este mi testamento... .

Pedro Zapata de Cardenas: Prominence in Isolation as a Purveyor of Indulgences

The strongest example of identity premised on separation of one's body from the bodies of others with whom one would normally be associated, is provided by Pedro de Cardenas, who like Magdalena, has left the family tomb and chapel to be buried elsewhere. He says "it would have been a great consolation to me" to have been buried with my grandfather and my wife who are interred there and "with my children and grandchildren and descendants who in times to come will go their rest there".[24] He himself cannot be buried there, as there is no room in the High Chapel for the memorial plaque that is to record the perpetual jubilee granted to him by Pope Pius V in reward for his services to the Holy League at the Battle of Lepanto. According to the terms of this privilege, any one who comes to pray for his soul and the souls of his ancestors, descendants and all his family on the eve and the day of Nuestra Señora de la Concepcion will earn a plenary indulgence and remission from all their sins with every intercession that they ask for.[25]

Here we have reason to argue for an identity which demands, not mere separation, but a prominence in isolation that is otherwise unmatched in my sample of wills. Pedro Zapata de Cardenas is not so much separated from his family with respect to perpetual remembrance of his soul. As the primary recipient of a papal indulgence, he also has enough clout to gain access to a unique grave site, one that will be reserved for him and only him forever and ever. In brief, he has been granted license by the Padre General of the Franciscan Order to be buried in the hollow of an arch that is located in the area where the friars are buried, in the vicinity of the altar "where souls are taken out of purgatory".[26] The arch itself is located towards the sacristy on the right hand side of the altar, a most advantageous position from which to have one's soul released into Heaven a little sooner as we saw in Chapter Two. Pedro Zapata de Cardenas ensures that hanging the standard that he carried into battle from the highest top point above his tomb further immortalizes his identity in this life. With this, and a repeated injunction that no other bodies ever be allowed to be deposited or interred with his, "as the hollow of the arch cannot hold more than one body",[27] he ensures an individual identity in death that will remain intact and enduring.

---

[24] Pedro Zapata de Cardenas, 1606, AHPM, Prot. 2015, fols. 1750r.-1758v.
...Yten mando y quiero y es mi postrimera y ultima voluntad que aunque yo y los subcessores de mi casa tenemos entierro principal de la capilla mayor de la dicha yglesia y monasterio de San Francisco donde pudiera enterrarme y fuera gran consuelo para mi estarlo con Po Capata de Cardenas mi senor y aguelo y dona Dionisia de Castilla mi legitima mujer que alli estan enterrados y con mis hijos y nietos y descendientes que a largos tiempos yran a el, que por quanto en la dicha capilla mayor no ay sitio donde poder quedar ecripta memoria del jubileo perpetuo que nro muy santo Padre papa Pio Quinto me concedio quando fui a Roma despues de la battalla nabal de Lepanto por el servicio que en ella hice a la Santa Liga, para todas las personas que la vispera y dia de la concepcion de Nra Sra visitaren la dicha yglesia de San Francisco y alli rogaren a dios por mi y por mis difuntos que alli estan y por mis descendientos y toda mi familia tantas quantas veces lo hicieron ganan plenaria y indulgencia y remision de todos sus pecados que porque en la parte donde se entierran los frayles y donde esta el altar priviliado donde se sacan almas del purgatorio que es por donde se va a la sacristia a la mano derecha del alto altar ay un arco y el padre guardian de la dicha cassa con licencia del Reverendissimo padre comisario general de la dicha horden que para ello le dio en mi presencia me ha dado el dho arco desde agora para siempre xamas para mi solo.

Y sin que en el se pueda enterrar en ningun tiempo otra persona ninguna y dello se hico escriptura... quiero que mi cuerpo sea sepultado dentro del Hueco del dicho arco en la manera que yo lo dexe hecho y acabado. Y en lo mas alto de todo el estandarte que yo truje con la cavalleria espanola de la liga... y ruego y en cargo a mis hijos y nietos y todos los demas subcessores que fueron de mi y mayorazgos della que tengan muy particular cuidado de la conserbacion y reparo y hornato del dicho mi entierro y no consientan en ningun tiempo por ello ni por el dicho convento se de licencia para que ninguna otra persona, se pueda enterrar ni depositar en el demas de que el dicho hueco que tiene no es capaz mas de para un solo difunto... .

[25] Pedro Zapata de Cardenas, loc. cit.
[26] Pedro Zapata de Cardenas, loc. cit.
[27] Pedro Zapata de Cardenas, loc. cit.

The Interplay among Action, Identity, Space and Time: Eternity of Soul as Expressed in the Presence of the Body in a Given Set of Associations

Sometimes this identity is built upon by setting up for an act which involves "union" or burial in association with some person or category of persons outside one's own relations by blood or marriage. In all the examples covered below, a connection is made between the testator's identity and the space given over to both living and dead representatives of religious brotherhoods or communities. No special proximity to the saints associated with each order is suggested other than the implicit fact of burial in ground named for them. What seems to matter most is the maintenance of an association with an on-going group that need not be interrupted by the death of the testator, or, in some instances, by the displacement of the community to some other site.

Pedro de Olivares, Maria de Ochoa, Hernando de Miguel, Pedro Martinez and Diego Mester del Campo: Connecting with a Confraternity

Several testators wish to be laid in chapels designated for interment of members of the confraternities to which they belong. Pedro de Olivares wants a grave in the chapel of all souls, in the church of Santa Cruz because he is a brother there.[28] Likewise Maria de Ochoa, being a member of the third order of the Franciscans, wants to be buried in the chapel of the tertiaries in the monastery of San Francisco.[29] For his part, Hernando de Miguel elects to be buried next to the grave of a deceased companion of the lay brotherhood of Maria de las Angustias, in the chapel of the same name,[30] itself located in the Hospital de la Pasion.
Sometimes the space associated with a confraternity or a group of religious specialists extends beyond the confines of a chapel. Pedro Martinez and his wife wish to be buried in the Hospital of San Luis Rey de Francia, as their confraternity, also known as San Luis Rey de Francia, is sited there.[31] Along similar lines, Diego Mester del Campo, himself a chaplain of the house, asks the abbess of the monastery of Las Descalzas Reales for license to be buried where all the other chaplains have been interred.[32]

Cristobal de Ramos, Pedro Martinez and Maria Moya de Truchado: Moving with the Monastery

In the foregoing examples, the testator's continued self-identification as a member of a confraternity even in death is clear. In the examples that follow, the association is not based on membership in the religious community. What comes across is the desire to preserve one's burial in the environs of the living, so much so that if the locale of the community should be changed from one building to another, then so shall the preferred site of burial. Cristobal de Ramos says that if he dies in Madrid, he wants to be buried in the convent of San Martin, currently occupied by discalced nuns of the order of St. Augustine. If the convent should be moved from its present location some time in the future, he insists that the prioress and the nuns are under obligation to "take my bones with them, at their expense" to the monastery where they have gone to live.[33]

---

[28] Pedro de Olivares, 1628, AHPM, Prot. 4025, fols. 1566r.-1567v.
...en la capilla de las animas de donde soy cofrade... .
[29] Maria de Ochoa, 1630, AHPM, Prot. 5535, fols. 448r.-451v.
...en la capilla de los tercios por quanto yo soy tercera de la orden... .
[30] Hernando de Miguel, 1580, AHPM, Prot. 1166, unpaginated.
...en la capilla de Maria de las Angustias e si se pudiere se pongan su sepultura junto a donde esta enterrado Jeronimo hermano mayor de la dicha cofradia mi companero difunto... .
[31] Pedro Martinez, 1624, AHPM, Prot. 4020, fols. 290r.-295v.
...en el Ospital de San Luis Rey de Francia, que esta en la calle que llaman del Postigo de San Martin como se va de la red de San Luis a mano izquierda en la sepultura de la dicha yglesia del que paresciere a qualquiera de nostros que sobreviviere, o a nuestras albaceas por ser como somos cofrades de los franceses que esta en el dicho hospital y en caso que el dicho ospital se mude de la parte donde esta a qualquiera otra que sea queremos ser alli enterrados... .
[32] Diego Mester del Campo, 1585, AHPM, Prot. 182, fols. 324r.-326v.
...quando yo fallesciere se suplique a la sra Abadesa deste Real Monasterio de las Descalzas sea servida de me dar licencia que yo sea sepultado en el entierro y sepultura donde se entierran y estan enterrados los capellanes desta casa y alli quiero ser sepultado... .
[33] Cristobal de Ramos, 1603, AHPM, Prot. 1437, fols. 125r.-129r.
...en el monesterio de San Martin, si muriere en esta villa...e digo si muriere en ella mi cuerpo sea sepoltado en el monesterio de las monjas recoletas agustinas descalzaas de esta dicha villa con que si se mudare el dicho monesterio en algun tiempo que la dicha priora, monjas e convento sean obligados a llevar a su costa mis guesos al monasterio donde se mudasen... .

For Pedro Martinez and his wife, place of burial is also contingent on going where the community of nuns or monks go, rather than claiming an eternal space within the confines of a building associated with the order itself. As we saw above, they wish to be buried in the Hospital de San Luis Rey de Francia. If the hospital should move from its present location on "the street called Postigo de San Martin" to some other place, they want to be buried there instead.[34] Similarly, Maria Moya de Truchado asks for a grave in the Capuchin convent which "at present stands at the cross of Moran, or where ever it may move to, in the part indicated by whoever may be abbess at the time".[35] In both of these examples, it is implied that the community could move before the testators die, in which case the prospective location of their graves will be altered to fit the new circumstance. Unlike Cristobal de Ramos, they do not ask that their bones be disinterred if the community should move again after they receive burial.

It is apparent from these examples that the body continues to be represented in death as an integral part of the testator's own self concept. Even when the flesh has rotted away and no semblance of the living person remains, the bones do not become anonymous. They are still "my bones". From the testator's (or anybody's) point of view then, this would suggest that personal identity is essentially unalterable even after death and decomposition of the body and the slow oblivion of the grave, which indicates that identity is outside the confines of physical space and time.

The Interplay among Action, Identity, Space and Time: The Continued Integration of Self with the Body even in Death

In the examples which follow, action may be directed in such a way that the testator's individual identity ultimately dissolves space and time via the apparent assumption that the soul remains integrated with the body, and is somehow anchored to the place where the body lies in its long rest before the Day of Judgement and the end of the world itself. The dominant image here is that of unbroken or continued integration despite the fact of the testator's death. We may think of the tree in leaf always, the evergreen tree, forever present and living, yet dying all at the same time.

Benigno Diaz, Ynes Sanchez and Catalina Diaz: Salvation of Self at Grave-Side

The texts under scrutiny here suggest that body and soul are not always distinguished as suffering a separate destiny in space and time. Both Benigno Diaz and Ynes Sanchez identify places where the bodies of loved ones are buried as loci for the salvation of the soul. Diaz wants to be buried with his parents in their grave "where...they receive their salvation".[36] Ynes Sanchez wills twenty maravedies to the church of San Julian in honor of her dead "who have received and await their salvation there".[37] Catalina Diaz may be translating something of the same sentiment into a temporal dimension when she asks that "they bury me at the hour that mass is sung".[38] For these people it seems, body and soul are so intimately connected, that space is rendered sacred and time turned into eternity at a grave site where the dead are still known to them.

---

[34] Pedro Martinez, loc. cit.
[35] Maria Moya de Truchado, 1626, AHPM, Prot. 4022, fols. 479r.-482r.
...en el convento de monjas capuchinas desta villa que al presente esta a la cruz de Moran o adonde se mudare, en la parte e lugar que la madre abadesa del en aquel tiempo fuere, señalare... .
[36] Benigno Diaz, 1458, AHPS, Prot. 9.3, fol. 8r.
...a donde dichos padres reciben su salvacion... .
[37] Ynes Sanchez, 1491, AHPS, Prot. 9.19, fol. 7r.
...que sea mi cuerpo sepultado en la yglesia o monesterio donde mi marido quisiere e mando a la dicha yglesia de Sant Julian por honra de los mis muertos que alla han rescibido e esperan su salvacion, veinte maravedies... .
[38] Catalina Diaz, 1458, AHPS, Prot. 9.3, fol. 13r.
...que me entierren en la sepultura donde esta enterrada Beatriz Alfonso, muger de Pedro Fernando Camargo y que me entierren a la hora de misa... .

Gabriello Permadera and Diego Sarmiento de Sotomayor: Integrity of Identity in All that Remains

If this be the case, it may also be argued that no action need be directed towards continued material and/ or ritual marking of the place where the body lies after the funeral ceremonies are over. No action need be made inevitable in a certain place at a particular time. In other words, personal identity need not be fractured by death. Gabriello Permadera appears to take the integrity of self for granted in describing the disposal of his body in burial. He offers his body "to the earth where it be deposited until the day of universal judgment, in a place that my wife Juana Bautista should choose".[39]

In another example, Diego Sarmiento de Sotomayor's claims to lordship over the chapel, church and town of Salvatierra are literally embodied by his judicious distribution of family skeletons. He wills that the remains of his parents, brothers and children be moved to his new monastery dedicated to San Diego, as soon as it is finished. He orders that his sister's bones be left in their original resting place "in the high chapel of the church of San Lorenzo of the said town as a sign that it belongs [insolidum] to its lord". He further adds that "no one else may ever be buried in any part there".[40] It is unclear whether he means just the chapel or the church itself. What is beyond doubt is his use of a body, not a grave or tomb, but an identifiable set of bones, to define a space and claim it for his own.

Ana de Melgarejo and Menzia de la Çerda y Mendoza: The Arbitrary Link between Identity and Action

We can safely say that identity does not have to be maintained: it is already in all that remains. Such an attitude need not be interpreted as lack of concern for the fate of oneself or one's body after death, or as a testator's failure to direct the action of others so that he or she secures a specific outcome. What the wills have to tell us is that any expectation that translates into a request for inaction is not synonymous with lack of action, though it may be manifest to us only as a lack of evidence.

Ana de Melgarejo provides us with a really solid example of a request for inaction. Should she die away from home, she does not want her body to be transferred at any cost. She says unequivocally, "if I die while away from the said town of Castillo de Garamuñoz, I want neither my body nor my bones to be transferred back to the said town, because it is my will that I remain wherever I am buried".[41]

The same may be said for any expectation that translates into a request for action that effects a transformation in space and time without material correspondence. Where a transfer of ones' body is effected in order to stay close to someone in particular, the place where the body of that loved one once lay is not merely empty; it is devoid of his or her presence. The transformation in space and time that I refer to above is effected, not just by moving bodies from one place to another, but by the knowledge of the presence or the absence of the body of the other person in relation to ones' own, exactly as it is in life. Mençia de la Çerda y Mendoza makes this abundantly clear when she says that she wants to be laid next to her husband "in the church of the town of Chinchon". She adds that when "they take him over to the new church, I order that they also take me and put me next to his grave, because it is my will that my body always be buried next to the Count, who is my lord and husband".[42]

---

[39] Gabriello Permadera, 1577, AHPM, Prot. 778, fols. 174r.-175v.
...el cuerpo ofrezco a la tierra donde esta depositado hasta el dia del universal juizio en la parte e lugar que paresciere y ordenare Juana de Bautista mi muger... .

[40] Diego Sarmiento de Sotomayor, 1613, AHPM, Prot. 2024, fols. 250r.-257v.
...mando que con toda perfeccion se acabe el monesterio de San Diego que voi acuerdo conforme a la traca y capitulaciones hechas y se muden los huesos de mis padres, hijos, hermanos y mios a la boveda y entierro que en el se acequedando solos los de mi hermana Dona Beatriz en la capilla maior de la yglesia de San Lorenzo desta dicha villa [de Salvatierra], en senal y prenda de que es insolidum de los senores della, y no tener otra persona en ella parte ninguna y aberla mi hermana dotado de dos capellanias perpetuas de que yo y mis sucesores somos patrones, y que de la obra del monasterio arriba referida no se alze mano por ningun caso, ni lo consienta mi hijo Garcia asta que se concluia de la suerte que esta dicho por que demas de ser la obra tal y tan santa autorica muebo su lugar, y cumple con la voluntad de sus abuelos y padres, y espero en Dios que por ella a de usar con el, y con su casa de grandes misericordias, y tenerla de mis pecados... .

[41] Ana de Melgarejo, 1583, AHPM, Prot. 180, unpaginated.
...si muriere en Castillo de Garamunoz, me entierren en la yglesia de San Juan de la dicha villa junto a las gradas de la capilla mayor, en la sepultura de mi tio Sanz de Olivares; y si muriere en otro lugar donde quisieren el sr. Geronimo Pinar de Zuniga o qualquier de los testamentarios e quiero que si muriese fuera de la dicha villa del Castillo, que mi cuerpo y guesos no sean trasladados a la dicha villa porque mi voluntad es que me quede donde fuera enterrada... .

[42] Mençia de la Çerda y Mendoza, 1584, AHPM, Prot. 181, fols. 17r.-20r.
...junto al conde en la yglesia de la villa de Chinchon, y quando lo pasaren a la nueva yglesia mando que tambien me pasen a mi, y me pongan junto a su sepultura, porque es mi voluntad que mi cuerpo este siempre sepultado junto al conde mi senor y marido... .

In closing, I would like to emphasize that the wills have allowed us to explore archaeology at its truest beginnings by starting with the individual as actor, creator and primary user of the evidence that he or she produces. All action is rooted in the relationship between individual identity and space and time, a relationship that we have touched upon in discussion of particular examples of text in the present chapter. I believe that in making such a connection I have made a positive contribution to the growing awareness among archaeologists that some concept of the individual as "prime mover" in the formation of any archaeological site is at the very heart of our discipline. I have also tried to show that such awareness need not be limited to general covering statements, but may in fact render new interpretative possibilities for what at first glance seems to be more of the same stale old stuff.

CHAPTER 7. CONCLUSION

A Summary of Approach and Content

The will has taken center stage both as document and as the remaining embodiment of an individual's personal will in every single one of the foregoing chapters to varying degrees, depending upon the angle at which our sights have been trained on the question of burial location. Such a layered approach has allowed me to explore content, mode of expression and action while never straying from the living words of men and women dead so long ago, as set before me on the pages of their wills. My intention has been to provide concrete examples of how such a record so intimately tied to the life and death of a human being neither singular nor famous, allows us to reach the core of archaeological interpretation in its truest, most pragmatic form. In my understanding, the heart of our endeavor here may be summed up by asking: "how do we relate the graves, bones and artifacts that we unearth from the ground to the individuals who left them there in ways that are consistent with the evidence at hand?"

My initial approach was to draw upon the similarities and differences between what we would expect to find upon excavation of a Christian burial and the information contained in a will regarding the same. I discussed artifacts, skeletal remains, their patterning and distribution, as reported for various Spanish medieval sites insofar as they are paralleled, or not, by accounts of the disposition of the body for burial and material indications of the grave site, as documented in the wills and vice versa. My conclusion was that neither set of information complemented the other directly as I had originally envisioned. I could no longer see either source as a template for the other.

Instead of changing topic, I simply shifted my focus to consider both the archaeological and historical data as foils. This strategy permitted me to set parameters on archaeological inference with respect to extrapolations of mind and meaning from limited historical evidence in preparation for my use and exposition of texts in the chapters to follow.

My new perspective also prompted an acute awareness that all data, regardless of their provenance, are constructs of one sort or another. Both the structure and the content of Chapters 4, 5 and 6 are informed and intimately associated with one another on the strength of this idea. It is, in some respects, the keystone of my work as it now stands. In Chapter 4, the nature of the construct is easy to trace, as it is expressed in a study of the contrast between the vocabularies that archaeologists and testators use to describe space and location in reference to the necessity of finding a grave. The interplay between criteria of recognition, based on experience and criteria of representation, derived from built-in assumptions, allows us to create a solid picture of both the archaeologists' and the testators' essential understanding of space and location as well. We are lead to a new construct of knowledge by a focus on specific examples of text, without need of recourse to larger abstractions.

The shift of old parameters on what is understood to be space and location via close study of the texts of the wills became a touchstone for a new way of seeing things. In Chapters 5 and 6, the will is understood as a commitment on the part of both testator and executors to prospective action on behalf of the former upon his or her death. It is created on the assumption of action and identity in the present tense, though it references a person's past and future. Seen in this light, the will as document is indeed inextricably aligned with personal will.

My Work is Embedded in an Archaeological Perspective

The real connection between human will and the expression of that will as an artifact, a document that can be read and acted upon by others, allows me to embed all subsequent discussion of action and identity in Chapters 5 and 6 in a truly archaeological perspective. I look at how the very stuff of archaeology, the bones, graves and artifacts inferred from references in the wills, may be related to the men and women who lived, died and left wills in Madrid and Seville four to five centuries ago in a holistic way. Their requests regarding the disposition of their bodies, the whereabouts and identification of their graves and the rites of remembrance for their souls, give us a window on the process by which both material and non-material constituents of objects, spaces, and mortal remains may be articulated by individual action.

Seeing the process at work, as it were, in the words of the testators themselves, gives us a model by which we may extend the scope of archaeological interpretation of grave sites in almost any cultural context should we chose to do so. We have enough information here, to see that individual identity at the grave site can be put together in any number of different ways.

As we have seen, identity is an individual construct, conveyed to others by means of explicit associations or not, and in wholly material forms or not. As such it may have a direct bearing on our interpretations of the material evidence that we do see in excavation - we may expect to see gravestones with epitaphs, which indicate that bones lie beneath, rather than an urn full of ashes, for example. The use of wills as sources for confirmation of material patterning is appropriate where one has excavated material to work with, which I have not. Given my archaeological training and the unique opportunity to work with such a large sample of documents however, I wanted to take things one step further.

I emphasize the material and extra-material evidence of individual identity mentioned in a will. Identity gives us great insight into the range of action and meaning that someone once invested in what we may only see as bones, irrespective of what survives and what does not. Herein lies the originality of my research for and from within an archaeological perspective - nothing is missing from what remains when we have artifacts - in my case, the wills - that we know how to interpret in order to build our understanding of the people who created them.

How the Information Derived from Wills can be Related to Archaeological Interpretation

Can the relationship between my findings and the possibilities for interpreting the archaeological record be made more explicit? The answer is "yes" and "no." If by "explicit," we mean expanding the range of possibilities for interpretation of the burial evidence, the answer is "yes". If we mean providing information that can help archaeologists to infer what patterning may exist among graves in a church or cemetery, the answer is far more equivocal.

Why? - Because a major implication of my research is identity - that is, the individual's construction of self - matters in determining the treatment of the body after death. My research has also shown how critical the concept of space is in the formation of identity, but in this case space and its correlates, such as rituals to be carried out in a particular place, are subsumed or "dictated" by identity, rather than the other way around.

This could mean big trouble for archaeology, since archaeologists prioritize space and wherever possible ignore the individual as something that merely produces "noise" when we try to determine patterns. My research shows that space and individual identity are inextricably linked.

The Implications of My Study for Archaeological Interpretation

So how can my research help in archaeological interpretation? First and foremost, it makes clear that in the study of any cemetery or group of burials, whatever patterns we determine will only form part of a larger picture. Culture, for example may tell us that children are rarely buried close to the altar; or that children in frontier regions like the area in which Tipu is located, were not baptized as infants, simply because an individual who had the authority to baptize made the rounds only infrequently, so that we might expect to find few infant burials in consecrated ground if at all. To this extent, cultural or religious practices might be easily reflected in particular patterns in the cemetery.

What the wills make clear is the amazing amount of creativity and range of choice displayed in an individual's interpretation of death and burial, even within the Christian cultural religious context. This was certainly not expected, simply because I had not anticipated that individuals would feel so strongly about their own identity after death. But it is this incredible drive to preserve identity (in addition of course to trying to use whatever power is at hand to carve out a place in the afterlife) that propels the choices made about burial placement and rituals.

At first this may seem only to complicate matters, but in fact, when we think of Tipu, it draws us closer to the Maya. We have always looked at ourselves as being separated from them by an enormous cultural gap, but we can now assume with some assurance, I think, that identity, too, must be considered to have influenced any individual Maya's decisions about burial. From Tipu we see variety in the kinds of personal adornments worn by individuals in death. We see mothers buried with children. We even see grave goods, as in the case of the adolescent child buried near the altar with a thurible, a Christian-style censer (Graham 1989).

The standard archaeological interpretation might be that these accouterments reflect the individual's social status. (This may be because the concept of social status, by being "social" rather than "individual," lends itself to patterning). I am not saying that social status may not indeed inform one dimension of this choice of accoutrements. Rather, my research makes it absolutely clear that the individual's concept of himself as an actor in controlling his passage from life to death - and in how living people will be thinking about him after his death - also influence where and how he is placed in burial.

Therefore although we cannot know what an individual was thinking, we cannot deny that his concern with his identity and his passage to the afterlife is not important. How might this help us in archaeology?

Well, we might consider that those individual burials that are found in more public spaces, such as doorways or near internal church furniture such as Holy Water stoups or baptismal fonts, might be more concerned than others with keeping their memories alive after death. We cannot be sure of this, or at least not as sure as we might be if we could show that individuals buried in a particular zone all wore readable adornments of a particular status. Rosary beads from Tipu are an example of such readable adornments, as they are known from documentary sources to be given to caciques (Graham 1993).

However, just entertaining the idea that individual identities structured burial placement compels us to consider the role of preserving identity after death as a key factor in that burial placement. We may even be able to propose where particular notions of identity (wanting rituals conducted at one's burial, for example) might be physically manifested - as I noted above, such an emphasis suggests a greater likelihood of burial in a more public, or well traveled area of the church. Alternatively, it could also be manifested in an area accessible only to a privileged few, as would be the case with individuals who wanted masses said in a private chapel, to return to an example taken from the Christian context of the wills.

A Final Coda

Such has been the trajectory of my thoughts on the subject of wills and what they may or may not tell us about graves and burial location, belief and action. In the course of the journey my own understanding has undergone a complete metamorphosis. I count it as a great contribution if I have also conveyed the same sense of excitement, involvement and discovery to all who read this work.

APPENDIX 1

TABLE 1

NUMBER OF TESTATORS WHO REQUEST BURIAL IN EACH NAMED CHURCH IN MADRID

Church	Number
San Gines	140
Santa Cruz	80
San Miguel de los Otoes	53
Santa Maria del Almudena	48
Santiago	34
San Andres	33
San Yuste	31
San Martin	29
San Sebastian	28
San Juan	27
San Pedro	25
San Salvador	18
San Luis	8
San Nicolas	5
San Gil	4
San Myllan	2
Casa de los Menores del Espiritu Santo	1

TABLE 2

NUMBER OF TESTATORS WHO REQUEST BURIAL IN EACH NAMED MONASTERY IN MADRID

Monastery	Number
San Francisco	60
Nuestra Señora de la Victoria	31
San Felipe	21
Nuestra Señora del Carmen	21
Nuestra Señora de la Concepción	18
La Santissima Trinidad	17
San Gerónimo	15
San Martin	15
Nuestra Señora de la Merced	12
Santo Domingo	10
Santa Clara	9
Caballero de Gracia	6
Recoletos Agustinos	4
San Basilio	3
Nuestra Señora de Lorito	3
San Hermenegildo	2
Nuestra Señora de Atocha	2
Las Descalzas Reales	2
Santa Barbara	2
Santa Ana	1
Santa Ysabel La Real	1
La Encarnación	1
Las Arrepentidas	1
Los Angeles	1

TABLE 3

**NUMBER OF TESTATORS WHO REQUEST BURIAL IN EACH
NAMED CHURCH IN SEVILLE**

Church	Number
San Llorente	13
San Vicente	13
San Miguel	11
San Salvador	11
Santa María la Mayor	9
San Andres	8
Santa Catalina	6
San Esteban	5
San Marcos	5
San Julian	5
San Gil	5
Omnium Sanctorum	5
San Juan de la Palma	3
Santa Marina	3
San Roman	3
San Pedro	2
San Nicolas	1
Santiago el Nuevo	1

TABLE 4

**NUMBER OF TESTATORS WHO REQUEST BURIAL IN EACH
NAMED MONASTERY IN SEVILLE**

Monastery	Number
San Francisco	20
Santa María de La Merced	11
San Pablo	8
Santa María del Carmen	3
Santa María de Las Cuevas	3
San Gerónimo	2
San Agustín	2
Santo Domingo	1
Santa Clara	1
Santiago de La Espada	1

TABLE 5

NUMBER OF TESTATORS WHO REQUEST BURIAL WITHIN A CHURCH OR MONASTERY SETTING

Burial within a church or monastery setting	Number
inside the church or monastery	202
inside or in the vicinity of a chapel	112
in the vicinity of an altar	46
inside or in the vicinity of a choir	24
in the vicinity of the grave of a friend	21
in the vicinity of the stoup of Holy Water	18
in the vicinity of one or more doorways	16
inside or in the vicinity of a nave	11
in the vicinity of space around the altar	6
outside in the monastery cloister	6
in the vicinity of incidental features	5
outside in the church cemetery	4

TABLE 6

**NUMBER OF TESTATORS WHO REQUEST BURIAL IN A
HABIT OF ONE OF THE REGULAR ORDERS**

Habit	Number
San Francisco	288
Santo Domingo	14
Nuestra Señora del Carmen	12
San Gerónimo	3
San Francisco de Paula	3
Nuestra Señora de La Merced	2
La Santíssima Trinidad	1

TABLE 7

**NUMBER OF TESTATORS WHO REQUEST BURIAL IN A
SECULAR HABIT**

Habit	Number
in the habit of a priest	17
in the habit of a lay confraternity	11
in the habit of a military order	2

APPENDIX 2. A SAMPLE WILL

A TRANSCRIPTION OF THE SAMPLE WILL

Only the first page of the will is shown. (Maria de Ribadeneyra y Castilla, 1549, AHPM, Prot. 144, fols. 517r.-v.) Slash marks show where one line begins and another ends in the original text. Italics correspond with abbreviated words. Capitalization, punctuation and the use of accents follow the usage in the document itself.

Yn dey nomine Amen porque no ay cosa mas çierta q*ue* la /muerte ni mas ynçyerta que la ora y por esto todo fiel y/catolico xpiano debe estar prevenido en tener cuenta con su/conçiencia por ende quiero que sepan quantos esta mi ca*rta* /de testamento vieren como yo doña/ maria de rribadeneyra y de castilla hija legitima de los/*señore*s illus*trados* juan de rribadeneyra y de doña ysabel de cast*illa*/mys señores padres que ayan santa gloria estando sana del /cuerpo y en mi entero juyzio y entendim*iento* qual dios n*uest*ro s*eñor*/fue servido de me le dar creyendolo que tiene y cree la sancta/madre yglesia de rroma hago y ordeno my testamento y/postrimera voluntad en la forma siguiente/

primeramente encomiendo mi anima a dios que la crio y rre/dimio por su preçiosa sangre y suplico a la vigen sin/... n*uest*ra señora sancta maria su madre sea mi abo/gada y quando dios sea servido de me llevar de esta p*re*/sentevida ofrezca y rrepresente my anima ante el benditissimo percatam*ient*o de n*uest*ro senor/

yten mando mi cuerpo a la tierra de donde fue formado/y quiero que sea sepultado en la yglesia de señor Santiago en la /capilla de mis señores padres y abuelos/

yten mando q*ue* aconpañen mi cuerpo la cruz y clerigos de Santi/ago y de san juan y les den lo acostumbrado/

yten mando que se digan por my anima çien misas y por las/ de mis señores padres y abuelos otros çiento la mitad/ en la d*ic*ha capilla y la otra mitad en los monesterios de/n*uest*ra señora de atocha y san fran*cisc*o donde a mis albaçeas les/paresçiere e q*ue* se digan con toda brevedad/

yten m*an*do que de mis bienes se doten dos misas en la capi/lla de mis señores padres cada semana por ellos y por mi/y por los debidos y proximos q*ue* mas neçesidad tuvieren... .

APPENDIX 3. ILLUSTRATIONS

Fig. 1. A plan of the church of San Gerónimo, Madrid, by Marina Pinto. Data from Orso 1989, Fig. 2. and Varela 1990, Fig. 16

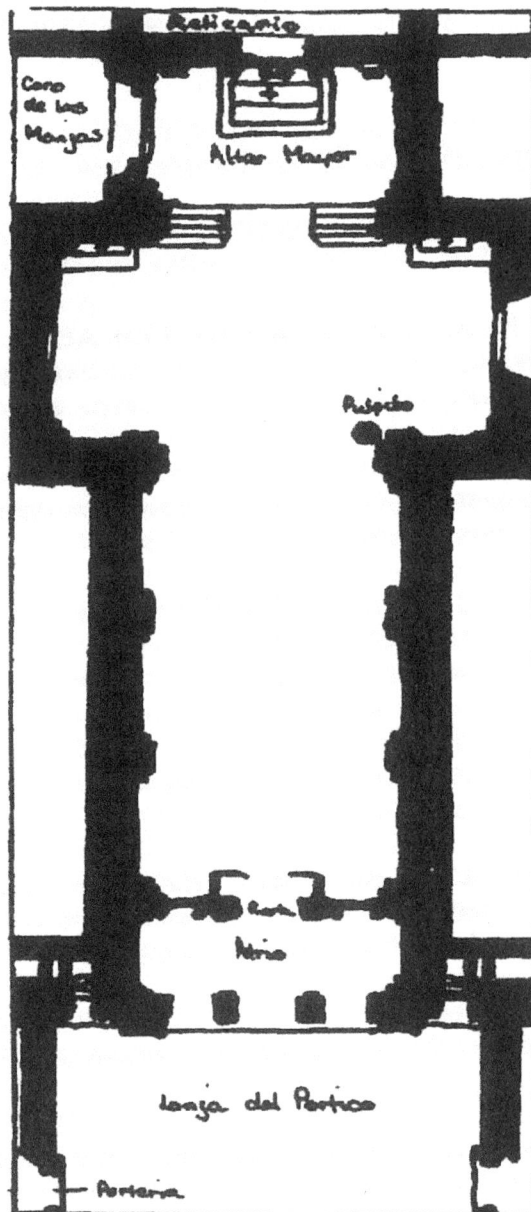

Fig. 2. A plan of the convent of La Encarnación, Madrid, by Marina Pinto. Data from Orso 1989, Fig. 55 and Varela 1990, Fig. 41

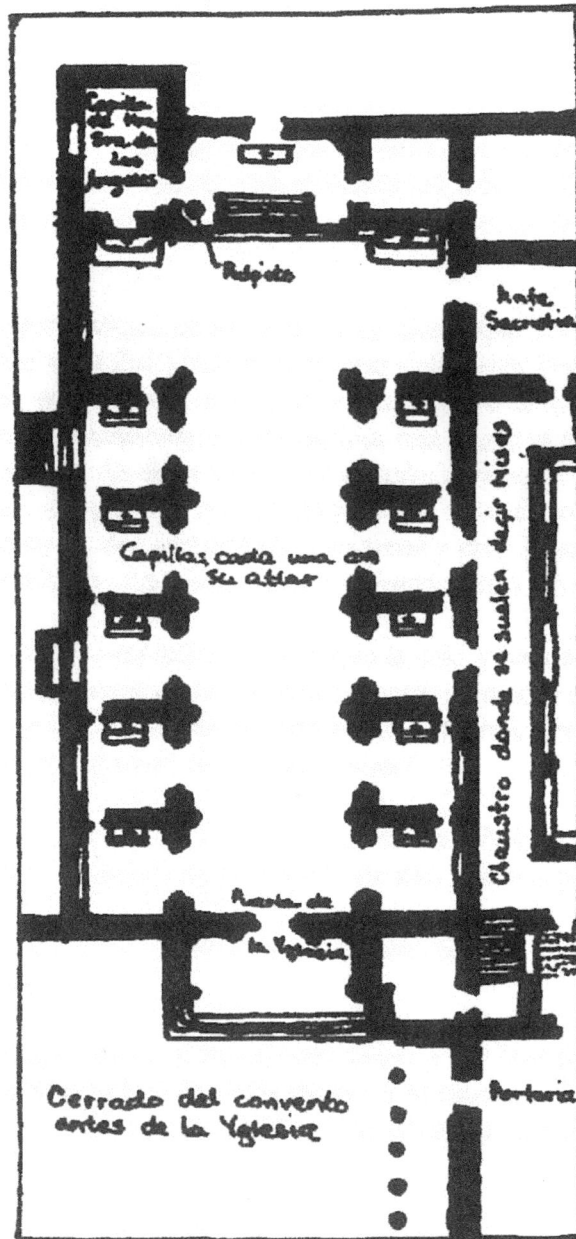

REFERENCES CITED

Argente Oliver, J. L. et. al. 1980 Tiermes 1. Excavaciones Arqueológicas en España: Memorias 3: 252-363

Ariès, Phillippe 1974 Western Attitudes Towards Death. London, P.M. Ranum.

Bango Torviso, Isidro 1981 Iglesia de San Martin de Valdilecha. Madrid, Diputación Provincial de Madrid.

Bertrán Roigé, Prim 1982 Hallazgo de Sepulturas Antropomorfas y de Una Ollita Gris en Bergus. Acta Historica et Archaeologia Medievalia 3:173-183.

Beresford, Maurice, and John Hurst 1991 Wharram Percy. New Haven, Yale University Press.

Bottomley, Frank 1978 The Church Explorer's Guide to Symbols and Their Meaning. London, Kaye and Ward Ltd.

de la Casa Martinez, Carlos et.al. 1985 Agreda Medieval 1. Noticiario Arqueológico Hispalense 26:215-331.

Colvin, Howard 1991 Architecture and the After-Life. New Haven, Yale University Press.

Christian, William A., Jr. 1981 Local Religion in Sixteenth Century Spain. Princeton, Princeton University Press.

Deagan, Kathleen 1983 Spanish St. Augustine. New York, Academic Press.

Delgado Valero, Clara 1988 Excavaciones en la Iglesia de San Lorenzo. Noticiario Arqueológico Hispalense 29:213-363.

Deetz, James 1977 In Small Things Forgotten. New York, Anchor Press.

Durán Sanpere, A., and J. M. Millás Vallicrosa 1947 Una Necropolis Judaica en el Montjuich de Barcelona. Sefarad 7:231-259.

Durandus, William The Symbolism of Churches and Church Ornaments. Translated by John Mason Neale and Benjamin Webb. New York, Charles Scribner's Sons.

Eire, Carlos M. N. 1995 From Madrid to Purgatory. Cambridge, Cambridge University Press.

Fernández González, Jorge Juan 1981. Excavaciones Medievales en Valeria. Cuenca, Diputación Provincial de Cuenca.

Fernández Nanclares, Alejandro Necropolis Medieval de "La Lámpara", Arroyo de la Encomienda (Valladolid). Noticiario Arqueológico Hispalense 24:389-413.

García Gallo, A. 1977 Del Testamento Romano al Medieval, Las Lineas de Su Evolución en España. Anuario de Historia del Derecho Español 47:425-497.

García Tomás, R. Gimeno et. al. 1983 La Necropolis Medieval de Tordesillas (Valladolid). Noticiario Arqueológico Hispalense 8:283-95.

Geary, Patrick J. 1978 Furta Sacra. Princeton, Princeton University Press.

Graham, Elizabeth Maya-Spanish Relations on a Colonial Frontier. Semi-annual Report to the Tinker Foundation. Photocopy.

Graham, Elizabeth, and Sharon Bennett 1989 The 1986-1987 Excavations at Negroman-Tipu, Belize. Photocopy.

de Juan García, Antonio Enterramientos Medievales en El Circo Romano de Toledo, Estudio Tipológico. In

Actas del Primer Congreso de Arqueología Medieval Española, 3:641-653. Huesca, Diputación Provincial de Aragón.

Jones, Grant D. 1988 Maya Resistance to Spanish Rule. Albuquerque, University of New Mexico Press.

Labe Valenzuela, Luis F. Necropolis Altomedieval en Biota (Zaragoza). In Actas del Primer Congreso de Arqueología Medieval Española, 5:245-259. Huesca, Diputación Provincial de Aragón.

Larren Izquierdo, Hortensia 1989 Excavaciones Arqueológicas en San Miguel de Escalada, (Leon). In Actas del Primer Congreso de Arqueología Medieval Española, 2:103-123. Huesca, Diputación Provincial de Aragón.

McIntosh, Jane 1986 The Practical Archaeologist. New York, The Paul Press Limited.

Merrifield, Ralph 1987 The Archaeology of Ritual and Magic. London, B.T. Batsford Ltd.

Navarro Palazón, Julio 1989 El Cementerio Islámico de San Nicolas de Murcia. In Actas del Primer Congreso de Arqueología Medieval Española, 4:7-47. Huesca, Diputación Provincial de Aragón.

Ollich i Castanyer, Imma 1982 Tipologia de les Tombes de la Necropolis Medieval de L'Esquerda, (Osona). Acta Historica et Archaeologia Medievalia Annex 1:105-147.

Orlandis, José 1976 La Iglesia en la España Visigótica y Medieval. Pamplona, Ediciones Universidad de Navarra S.A.

Orso, Steven N. 1989 Art and Death at the Spanish Hapsburg Court. Columbia, Universty of Missouri Press.

Puertas Tricas, Rafael 1982 Necropolis de los Hoyos de los Peñones (Alozaina, Málaga). Noticiario Arqueológico Hispalense 13: 247-303.

Ramos Fernández, Julián 1979 La Necropolis Medieval de las Mesas de Villaverde El Chorro, (Málaga).

Mainake 1:168-184.

Ripia, Juan de la 1674 Practica de Testamentos y Modos de Subceder. Cuenca, por Antonio Nuñez

Enriquez. Riu y Riu, Manuel 1974 La Necropolis y Poblado de La Torrecilla. Anuario de Estudios Medievales. 7-40.

Riu y Riu, Manuel 1982 Enterramientos Infantiles frente a las Puertas o en el Subsuelo de las Viviendas en la España Medieval (Siglos X al XIII). Acta Historica et Archaeologia Medievalia 3:185-200.

Rodwell, Warwick 1989 Church Archaeology. London, B.T. Batsford Ltd.

Varela, Javier 1990 La Muerte del Rey. Madrid, Turner Libros S.A.

Zamora Canellada, A. 1979 Datos en Torno a la Necropolis Medieval de San Juan de los Caballeros de Segovia. Noticiario Arqueológico Hispalense 6:581-606.